Oxford
September 1990

A POINT OF VIEW

A Point of View

Barry Took

Foreword by
Michael Palin

Duckworth

First published in 1990 by
Gerald Duckworth & Co. Ltd.
The Old Piano Factory
43 Gloucester Crescent, London NW1

ISBN 0 7156 2348 6

British Library Cataloguing in Publication Data

Took, Barry
A point of view.
1. Comedy – Biographies
I. Title
791.092

ISBN 0–7156–2348–6

Photoset in North Wales by
Derek Doyle & Associates, Mold, Clwyd.
Printed in Great Britain by
Redwood Press Limited, Melksham

Contents

Foreword
by Michael Palin

When I was young I wanted to be Barry Took. My friend wanted to be Marty Feldman. Sometimes we switched roles. We weren't *that* fussy so long as we might one day have our names, like theirs, announced on the radio or rolled by on the television over the intoxicating sound of audiences laughing themselves silly. *The Army Game, Bootsie and Snudge, Round the Horne* – to name, as they say, but a few – aroused our admiration and envy. What sort of people must they be who could write funny lines with such proficiency and profligacy? I pictured Barry as a small, nervous, infectiously friendly man with bulging eyes. My friend, with, I thought at the time, a disappointing lack of imagination, saw Marty Feldman as a tall, urbane figure with a merry twinkle in the eye – a cross between Jacques Tati and the head of the World Bank. Many years later, by one of those wild and improbable strokes of fate that make life almost worth the bother, my distant hero became a good friend and I realised Barry wasn't small at all.

What was even more unexpected was that I discovered, twenty years on, that I, the spotty Sheffield schoolboy who actually listened to writing credits, could make Barry Took laugh. Mind you, almost anything can make Barry Took laugh. His generosity with mirth is legendary. I've seen his face look solemn marginally fewer times than I've seen total eclipses of the sun. He radiates receptivity to humour. He's one of the few people I know who actually says 'hee-hee!' In Barry's humour are all the properties – malice, glee, joy, absurdity, love and hate – harmoniously balanced.

Po-faced sociologists without a glint of humour may try to

explain laughter, but when Barry Took speaks about the arcane process people listen. Well, I do anyway. I've listened to Barry ever since he told Terry Jones and myself that we could write comedy. I've listened to Barry ever since he told us that if we got together with certain people called Cleese, Chapman, Idle and Gilliam we could write even better comedy, and I listen to Barry now when he tells me to give up comedy and concentrate on writing forewords for his books. I listen because of his experience, because of his unapologetic enthusiasm for good work, and because, dammit, he knows so much and says it so well.

I can think of no one better qualified than Barry to write his autobiography.

February 1990 Michael Palin

Introduction

In the past forty years I have been involved in entertainment as a scriptwriter, stage, radio and television performer, dance band musician, stage hand, cinema projectionist, adviser to the BBC's Comedy department, lecturer on comedy scriptwriting, journalist, a voice-over in commercials, maker of promotional videos and sound tapes, song writer, director of intimate revue, tv producer, after-dinner speaker and many other things besides. I have come to feel like a doctor in general practice. The phone rings, I answer it and whatever the 'ailment' I turn out and try to solve the patient's problem.

Not always successfully, I might add, and looking back I see my career littered with disasters. Mercifully people only want to remember success, and quickly forget flops.

What I have tried to do in this book is to chronicle the moments in my life which I think are most significant to me and most likely to interest the casual reader.

To go into my career in minute detail would be a long and tedious business, a catalogue of radio and tv shows good and bad, of protégés who have succeeded and others who have failed, of essays into consultancies in tv companies which have proved so negative that I can't even remember the names of the people I've worked for.

Then there are the scripts written and rejected, and my adventures since taking up golf which are only of interest to me. I haven't even written about my ten years plus of chairing the *News Quiz* on BBC Radio 4 which has a devoted following and which I have come to enjoy almost more than anything else I've done. But what more can I say than that I've enjoyed it, and leave it at that?

This book then is not a catalogue of triumphs but a record of events and people who (or which, as the case may be) have intrigued, amused or influenced me.

It's not easy to write about oneself. What is tedious to me may be interesting to the reader (and all too often vice versa) so why attempt autobiography at all?

Can't you wait, people think, until you are dead, or at least senile, and then let some unbiased hand write the extended obituary that all biographies inevitably are?

Well, the reason I have written this is that since only I know what it is like to be me, for what that is worth, only I can tell the story which has contained, for me, scarcely a dull moment.

1

Euston

I don't remember three out of my four grandparents, they having gone to meet their maker before I was conscious of them. I do remember my mother's mother, an imperious, cantankerous old biddy who smelled of mothballs and who treated her unmarried daughter, my mother's older sister, as a personal servant.

'Unmarried' was something of a theme on my mother's side of the family, since she discovered in her late teens that the man she had called father all her life wasn't – but that Joe, the lodger, was. She was deeply shaken by the news when she did learn the truth but came to accept its inevitability. In the late-Victorian, early-Edwardian period divorce was impossibly difficult and expensive for working-class people, and so the live-in 'lodger' came to be the acceptable substitute for a second husband. What the man who was theoretically my grandfather made of it I can't say, but his substitute managed to sire six children, of which my mother, Kate Louie Rose, was the youngest; and the home was, by all accounts, a happy one.

Among my uncles and aunts were some curiosities. My Aunt Hetty, married to my mother's brother George, wore false teeth but would take them out when she chatted to anyone, holding the dentures in her hand and popping them back in her mouth when the conversation was over.

My Uncles Joe and Jack, married respectively to Moss and Maud, were both fine carpenters, came out of the Navy in 1918 and went to work at the Handley Page aircraft factory in Cricklewood. Later, when the housing boom of the twenties and thirties created the vast sprawling suburbs of north London, Joe and Jack decided to become builders. ('Jerry builders' my father rather dismissively called them, a term of the time for the slap-'em-up-quick-and-don't-take-down-the-scaffolding-until-the-wallpaper-is-up school of house construction.)

For a while all was well, but then it was revealed that Jack was heavily in debt and had gone bankrupt. Shortly after he died of a heart attack. Joe continued to prosper.

My Uncle Will, the oldest of the six children, was a violinist playing in the pit orchestras of the silent picture palaces until, with the coming of talkies, he was thrown out of work. He had a tough struggle for some years, until at last he found a regular job in the pit orchestra of the London Palladium and later on in Charles Shadwell's radio orchestra.

My Auntie Doll never married, and acted as a drudge for her mother until the old girl's death eventually liberated her.

As in any family, most of my relatives had personal idiosyncrasies. My Aunt Maud, for instance, was very deaf and when she chose could opt out of any conversation that bored her by switching off her hearing aid. The memory of Hetty, teeth in hand, shouting some item of family news to Maud who couldn't hear a word was a comic moment I treasure.

My father's family was poor but conventional. Alfred and Eliza Took lived in Camberwell, had six children, three girls, three boys, who all prospered and lived well and themselves had children who were healthy and bright and became in time thoroughly middle-class. My father, like my mother, was the youngest of the family, and they met when my father, who served in the Navy in the First World War, made friends with my uncles, who served on board the same ship, a light cruiser HMS *Champion*. They went through the Battle of Jutland together, and later on leave the Cox boys (Cox was my mother's maiden name) took Charles William Took, my father, then a handsome young petty officer, home to meet their family.

For Kate and Charlie – thanks to Charlie Chaplin, in those days anyone called Charles became known as Charlie – it was love at first sight, and after the war when my father left the Navy and had settled into a civilian job, they married and made their home in Muswell Hill in north London. In 1924 their first child,

Philip, arrived, and in 1928 I appeared.

My father's father, Alfred, was an eccentric, restless man by all accounts and when sober was a brilliant metalworker, a craftsman of the old school, but all too often drank too much and as a result was frequently out of work.

At the time I was born he had retired, and when, on a bright June morning in 1928, news reached Camberwell that Kate and Charlie had had a second son, Grandfather Alfred was sent off to visit Muswell Hill and bring back news of the latest Took to appear on the scene. Forsaking public transport he walked the ten miles or so from Camberwell to 161 Victoria Road, N22, doubtless stopping off for refreshment en route. When he arrived my father greeted him and invited him upstairs to see Kate and the new baby. The old man declined, sat on the stairs until he'd got his breath back and after a brief chat with my father set off to Camberwell again – on foot.

When he arrived back home in Albany Road he was asked eagerly 'What's the baby's name?' He thought for a moment and said – 'Euston.' Why Euston? I suppose that possibly having taken a little too much refreshment at the various pubs along the way the name Barry had gone completely out of his head but he remembered passing the LMS Terminus at Euston and that name had stuck.

This story was, of course, told to me much later, but having a similar difficulty in remembering names I have sympathy with the old chap. After all, if you can call your daughter Victoria why not call your son Euston?

*

My father, who was a commercial traveller and later office manager in the grocery business, was, in his day, a first-class amateur footballer and cricketer, one of the first boy scouts, and a writer of the most beautiful Pitman shorthand. He was also an excellent carpenter, brick-maker and bricklayer and a keen and resourceful gardener. Although he had 'the work ethic' firmly fixed in his mind, he could on occasion let his hair down and entertain a family group with a panache that few of his business colleagues would have recognised. He had nicknames for various neighbours, calling one, who worked in some vague capacity at the Stock Exchange, 'the share pusher'. Another, a poorly individual with indifferent health, he described as 'drinking red ink' (some innocent medicine, I suppose). A third was called, without ceremony, 'that bloody old fool'. He was as terse with his own family, calling his two older brothers 'the white rats' on account of their prematurely grey hair, and his older sister, who was rather plain, 'Doggo'. His command of invective must have been considerable, working as he did in Smithfield Market, but he kept his language well under control at home. He was a courteous and polite man on most occasions, but I remember once standing with him at a bus stop. The bus drew up and a portly woman stepped off the bus and right onto my father's foot. The pain must have been excruciating and he gasped out an agonised 'Christ!' before remembering his manners, raising his hat and adding through clenched teeth, 'Madam.'

His great hates were the Western Brothers, a comic double act very popular in the thirties and forties, who posed as ex-public school men and exuded a world-weary manner while churning out topical songs of their own invention. My father's dislike of them arose from the fact that one (was it Kenneth or George? – it's hard to remember, as his name was really Ernie) had been engaged to my mother before my father had wooed and won her.

In later years, when the Western Brothers had become national favourites, she would comment wistfully and frequently on their happy relationship. This inevitably caused my father to become deeply irritated and denigrate the Western Brothers (who were, in fact, cousins) whenever possible.

In the end the act broke up, one Western 'Brother' died and the other, my mother's one-time lover, finished up running a tobacco and newspaper kiosk at Woking railway station ... to my father's entire satisfaction.

I suppose that this frail link with show business must have made me interested, albeit unconsciously, in the idea of entertaining, and the occasional glimpses of my father being extremely funny were something that clung to me – something that I *could* perhaps emulate. Frankly, I wasn't much good at anything else. My older brother was also good with his hands, made and flew model aeroplanes of his own design and constructed a variety of primitive radio sets. I shared none of my brother's skills or attributes and inherited none of my father's abilities. The truth is that from an early age I felt unwanted and a failure.

My mother, who had a great deal of intelligence, failed singularly to use it when she told me on one occasion, when I was about eight years old, 'Of course you weren't planned. We had never wanted a second child but these accidents do happen.' Then, perhaps realising this revelation must have been deeply disturbing to me, she added, 'Of course we were delighted when you *did* arrive. Only, you know how nervy your father is and he was worried as to whether we could afford two children. As it was, he had a nervous breakdown shortly after you were born. I had to take him away. That's why Phyllis looked after you so much when you were little.' This whole episode bit deeply. It's an awful thing to tell a child that it's not wanted, and implying that in some way I was responsible for my father's nervous breakdown really shattered my self-confidence.

The good thing to come out of the affair was that Phyllis, a sweet, gentle creature in her early twenties, was an excellent substitute mother. I owe my left-handedness to her as it was she who taught me to write and draw.

The simple truth of the situation was that my mother was devoted to her elder son, on whom she lavished much of her affection, and I was superfluous to her emotional needs.

For the rest of my childhood I had to fight for her attention and sought substitute families wherever I could: families I hoped would not see me as an accident.

I suppose my mother blurted out this unfortunate information while she was suffering from feelings of anger and frustration because, poor woman, she had neither skills as a housekeeper nor the will to make a life for herself outside the home.

Not for her the Women's Institute, evening classes or voluntary work; she preferred gossiping with friends and hated being a suburban housewife having to keep within a tiny housekeeping allowance.

My attitude to my mother who, like my father and my brother, has been dead for many years, is ambivalent. On the one hand she could be bright, cheerful and loving and was always ready for a chat. On the other, having no achievements of her own, she lived only for her sons' successes and sought to make capital for herself out of them, taking credit for my brother's or my own petty triumphs ('You take after me') and passing off our shortcomings as attributable to my father.

At the time, however, I was so steeped in my own sense of inferiority that it seemed perfectly natural that I was merely a reflection of my mother's superior ability. That said, I wasn't a whey-faced introvert, peering fretfully from behind the net curtains. The truth was that, from an early age, I was mischievous and adventurous – in short a pain in the neck.

When I was just eight I learned to swim by hurling myself into the deep end of the local swimming pool and struggling to the side. I learned to ride a bicycle (my brother's) on the same trial-and-error basis. I was always seeking to find out what things were and how they worked. Unfortunately, like the sorcerer's apprentice, I would start things that I couldn't finish.

When I was very young, cars and, particularly, lorries had an almost hypnotic fascination for me. When I was three I climbed into a grocery van parked outside our house while the driver made a delivery. The van was facing uphill on our rather steep road, and after testing the horn and wrestling with the steering wheel I released the handbrake. The van ran briskly backwards down the hill, across the mercifully empty main road, and came to a somewhat noisy rest jammed in the iron railings that surrounded the local school.

A year or so later I did precisely the same thing, this time to a laundry van which careered downhill and demolished a neighbour's garden wall. Don't ask me why I did it. The mystery is as impenetrable as my grandfather's curious stab at my Christian name.

*

By the time of the laundry van incident we had moved from Victoria Road, which my parents had rented, to a newly built 'modern' house in Winton Avenue, part of a new speculative building site in New Southgate which they bought for under £600! It wasn't big (three bedrooms plus usual amenities) but had a garden back and front and a view from the back of the house over some acres of allotments to the wide-open spaces of Muswell Hill Golf Club. When we moved in, the houses on the other side of the road were still being built and the road hadn't been made up, being merely an expanse of gravel, mud and potholes.

It was one of those that saved my life. Not yet five, I was fascinated by the building work going on so close to home and by the builders themselves, who seemed to come from another world. They made me a sort of mascot and were always happy to share their tea, brewed in a bucket and sweetened with condensed milk. However, on the day in question I dashed across the road to see my navvy friends and, not seeing the approaching car, I was run over. The car bounced me into a pothole and, although knocked unconscious, I escaped major injury. The motorist, who was more upset than I was, kindly drove my mother and me to the doctor, who pronounced me shaken but unstirred and, by and large, intact.

On the way back home I'm told I sang a popular song of the time, 'Ain't It Grand To Be Blooming Well Dead.'

In spite of my early adventures with motor transport, memories of my childhood are mainly of horse-drawn vehicles. The coalman, the milkman, and the baker all had horse-drawn vans, and there was a travelling grocery called Carwardines which was also horse-drawn and ground its way round the hills and dales of north London dispensing De Reske Minor cigarettes ('the ten-minute smoke for intelligent folk' the adverts said), Eiffel Tower pudding, Icilma face cream, Betox meat spread, Shippam's fish paste, Virol, Marmite, Zebo liquid grate polish, and other staples of our thirties existence. There were also door-to-door salesmen, generally ex-servicemen desperately scraping a living, and a lady who, I guess, was a war widow, known as the 'stocking woman', who turned up every week selling silk and lisle stockings door to door.

My mother welcomed these callers, who broke up the monotony of her day, and would stand and chat with them all. I don't think she bought much, but the callers seemed to enjoy these little gossips too as a break from the more usual 'Nothing today, thank you' and a slammed front door.

My mother's other relaxation was music. We had a piano which she played (badly) and which until the late thirties was the only decent piece of furniture we owned. In 1937 my father was promoted to be manager of the Smithfield branch of the Danish Bacon Company, where he'd been working for some years, and our standard of living shot up rapidly.

Until then we had always had a fortnight's holiday every year, but out of season and to small boarding houses or farms in Dorset. At Swanage railway station one year a taxi driver offered his services. My father declined. 'I know your sort,' the taxi man shouted. 'Plus-fours and no breakfast.' In other words poor but pretentious.

The truth was that we were never that hard up but my father had a morbid dread of being out of work and saved what money he could. We weren't a Pooteresque family putting on airs but poor as churchmice. We always had a 'daily' as my mother, small though our house was, couldn't cope with housework, and more often than not we had a car. One I remember particularly, a Hillman Minx, looked good but was a complete washout, forever breaking down, often barely out of sight of home. When my father finally lost patience with it and sold it he offered us the compensation of a weekly visit to one of the local music halls, either the Wood Green Empire or the Finsbury Park Empire.

Needless to say neither of these Palaces of Variety still exist, nor if they did would anyone patronise them, but in the late thirties a good variety bill was enchanting and the full houses greeted their favourites with uproarious delight.

My favourite, indeed every Londoner's favourite, at the time was Max Miller whose gaudy clothing and risqué patter made him unique. 'There'll never be another, lady,' he'd shout to some shrieking matron in the stalls, and he was quite right. When Max Miller finally retired the music halls had quietly died. In the 1930s, however, they thrived and added a touch of sparkle to our everyday lives.

Dressed in outrageous floral plus-fours, a multi-coloured overcoat with a white fur collar, golf socks, two-tone shoes and a rakish white homburg hat, and brandishing a walking stick with a huge cut-glass knob, Miller would swagger on to the stage, hang his overcoat on an (invisible) hook placed in the backcloth, and start his performance. It was a mixture of impudence, innuendo and brash sexuality. 'Look at that,' he'd say, twirling his cane so that the simulated knob twinkled in the spotlight. 'I'm filthy with money – I'm filthy without it too. A poem ... a little poem. Jack and Jill went up the hill, as bright as two cock linnets, Jill came down with half a crown, she hadn't been up two minutes.' And when the audience would scream with laughter he'd shout at the bellowing throng 'It's people like you who get me a bad name.' Then he'd produce two books, one from each pocket: one white, the other blue. He'd say, 'In the white book there's all the clever jokes – in the blue book there's all the others – which one do you want?' The audience would shout as one: 'The blue book, Max. The *BLUE* book.' It was a clever device that licensed Miller's more risqué patter.

Alas, not all the music hall turns had Miller's flair, and sitting through a mediocre variety bill of unfunny comedians, elderly jugglers and nasal tenors could be a tedious experience.

My father soon tired of these family outings and in fact bought another car, a Ford, which served us well and as far as I can remember never let us down. It was back to 'runs in the country', generally round the same few back lanes in Hertfordshire or, if lucky, to the charming village of Chipperfield to watch the locals playing cricket, or pick wild flowers, or just meander through the woods. My word, it was boring, and I'd avoid these outings whenever I could.

I preferred the urban delights of music hall and cinema, the wireless and reading comics. Comics in those days were full of reading matter and not just a few words to explain the pictures. Monday it was *The Adventure*, Tuesday *The Wizard* – I can't remember Wednesday – but Thursday brought *The Hotspur* and Friday *The Rover*. I devoured them all.

*

By 1938 it had become obvious to most people that the Spanish Civil War was only a prelude to World War Two, and having seen newsreels of the effects of the air raids on Guernica, and the classic film *Things to Come*, everyone was sure that war would start unannounced with a massive air raid.

Small wonder that when war did come, and with it the air raid warning, on the morning of 3 September 1939 I was, to my eternal shame, petrified with fear and shed tears generated by pure funk. For the rest of the war whether suffering the Blitz, V1s or V2s I was left unmoved and, in fact, rather enjoyed the excitement and never felt that bowel-trembling fear again until I developed 'mikefright' in my early broadcasting career.

Much to everyone's surprise I had, in the summer of 1939, passed the examination that would take me to the school where my brother flourished, Stationers, a minor public school, founded by the Stationers Company in the nineteenth century. Its traditions were liberal and literate, and I need hardly say that it no longer exists, having been swallowed up in a series of amalgamations, and is today submerged in a comprehensive in Tottenham. Even the site in Hornsey, on which the school stood, has been bulldozed and turned into public gardens where the illiterate can trade drugs and sniff glue to their hearts' content.

I was due to start my secondary education on 19 September 1939, but Hitler had an altogether different timetable and invaded Poland on 1 September. Living in an outer suburb of London evacuation was optional, although towards the centre of the capital it was obligatory. The Took family were not the only ones to suppose that war would be heralded by a sky black with enemy bombers. In reality after that first scare life continued as peacefully as in pre-war days as Hitler mopped up Poland and prepared for his next attack.

Britain was like a disturbed ants' nest. East End children were billeted on farm labourers' families, and country schools had to share facilities with their London counterparts. Almost everybody hated every aspect of the evacuation plan, and thousands drifted back to London and other big cities during late 1939 and 1940 to be back home in time for the Blitz of 1940–41. At the start of the war the non-evacuated part of Stationers was seconded to Minchenden School, a group of charming buildings set in the midst of playing fields in the salubrious London borough of Southgate. At first we had one morning's lessons per week. Later we had five afternoons per week, but as you can imagine it was a bad start to grammar-school life.

From the age of five i'd been to the local council school at Bounds Green where I'd fallen madly in love with my very first teacher, a pretty young woman who seemed to me a much more suitable person to be my mother than my real one was. Then my interest in school ebbed and flowed. If a teacher liked me and was encouraging I got good results, if not I didn't. One year I suffered the ignominy of being demoted to the B Stream. At the next exams I came top and was rewarded by my father dubbing me 'the king of the damned'. The next year, back in the A Stream, I was promised a cricket bat if I came in the first three in the end of term exams. I came third, and got the bat.

At Junior School I could sprint and hurdle, but being shortsighted and wearing spectacles from the age of nine, I was not very good at cricket and hopeless at soccer. My best friend in those pre-war years, and a canny footballer, was a Scots lad whose father, a printer, had been banished from his company's Aberdeen works to London. His name was Bill McIlwraith, and he is today a fine script writer and playwright with many series (including the Donald Sinden/Elaine Stritch comedy, *Two's Company*) to his credit.

I had few other close friends when I was a child, being even then somewhat of a loner. My constant companions were the shadowy figures up there on the big screen at the local cinemas and the many excellent radio performers whose voices you came to know as you knew those of your own family.

My favourite was Commander Stephen King-Hall, whose no nonsense chats were riveting and whose bluff signing-off phrase 'Be good but not so good that people will say "What's he been up to?" ' struck me at the time as the epitome of wit. Then there was the wonderful *Band Waggon* (and yes, Waggon was spelt with two g's) with Arthur Askey and Richard Murdoch in their imaginary flat on top of Broadcasting House, by far the funniest of pre-war broadcasters. Another popular favourite was Robb Wilton as Mr Muddlecombe JP, a dithering magistrate whose court cases were utter confusion, and as the thirties merged into the wartime forties Jack Warner became the star of *Garrison Theatre* with monologues, a catchphrase 'Mind my bike' and fictional letters from his brother Sid.

By this time Robb Wilton had stopped being Mr Muddlecombe

and broadcast a series of radio monologues describing life in the Home Guard, beginning invariably 'The day war broke out ...' My favourite routine was where Wilton was being twitted by his wife about the time he was wasting in the Home Guard whose HQ was the back room of a local pub.

> She said 'What are you actually going to do?' I said 'If Hitler invades it's my job to stop him.' She said 'But he won't come alone. There'll be hundreds of them. How will you know which one is Hitler?' I said 'I've got a tongue in my head.'

A wonderful example of how the British will reduce world-shattering events to the mundane level of domestic trivia. Seen as an ogre, Hitler was frightening. Seen as a joke, he just looked foolish; and although we know today that Hitler's Germany was unspeakably bestial it's surely better to go to war with a smile than with a scowl. Not that I'm saying I think war is a joke, and in Britain in 1940 it was kill or be killed.

*

The weather throughout that summer was glorious and as the RAF battled it out with the Luftwaffe over south-east England we exiled Stationers cycled to our temporary school in Southgate gazing up with awe and excitement as the vapour trails of the air battles over London made exotic white patterns in the pure blue sky. Britain, buoyed up by Churchill's rhetoric, went briskly to work to produce the guns and the planes that we were going to need, it seemed, pretty soon. All over the countryside brick and concrete pill-boxes were being constructed to defend the land against the coming invasion, while old men and young boys in the LDVs (Local Defence Volunteers, subsequently known as the Home Guard) drilled with carving knives tied to broomsticks and sat up to all hours making Molotov cocktails (named after the Russian Foreign Minister) – which consisted of a wick made of rags stuck into a milk bottle full of petrol – the idea being to light the 'wick' and drop the cocktail through the open hatch of an enemy tank, assuming that the enemy would obligingly leave the hatch open.

When the Battle of Britain had been won and the Luftwaffe

turned its attention to flattening London, Bristol, Coventry, Plymouth and the rest, my father was drafted by the Ministry of Food as a salvage officer, a job which meant that after every air raid on Central London and the docks he had to visit the bombed-out provision warehouses and canning factories to see what food was salvageable and what had to be destroyed. He was often among the first to visit the scene of the previous night's Blitz and soon became convinced that my mother, brother and I should leave London. Stationers School had been evacuated to Wisbech in Cambridgeshire, and thither we went, at first billeted on an uncomplaining bank manager and his family and later in half of a large house which we rented from and shared with a family called Green. It must be said that through late 1940 and most of 1941 life for the Took family was idyllic.

The house we shared had a large garden, an orchard and a pond big enough to skate on in winter and swim in in summer. The River Nene flowed past the front door – not immediately in front, you understand, but on the other side of the road and down a steep bank – and the garden backed onto a riding school.

My father visited at weekends when he was able, and for me it was paradise: cycling around the countryside, swimming, learning to ride, playing table tennis in the big hall of the house, climbing trees and, greatest of treats and thrills, watching an RAF dance band at close quarters playing for dancing in the local Corn Exchange. I'd gained entry to the dances (I was twelve at the time) by the ingenious method of asking the bandsmen if I could help to carry in their instruments, music stands and so on. They good-humouredly allowed me to and I stuck close to the bandstand all night. It was then that I determined that by some means, however devious, I would one day become a dance-band musician.

As the war progressed and it became clear, when Hitler invaded the USSR and later when the USA joined in, that Britain was not going to be invaded and that the Luftwaffe had been moved to the Russian front, my family along with many others moved back to London: my mother to the problems of a wartime housewife, my brother to the Chelsea Polytechnic to study Maths and Physics. I did not go with them but was billeted with a very nice family who agreed to look after me. I hated being left behind and behaved abominably to the family I was billeted on. After a few weeks of this misery I decided that I too would go to London. I cycled the twenty miles from Wisbech to Peterborough and in spite of having no money boarded the London train and then cycled from Kings Cross to our home in New Southgate.

It was shock horror all round, but I was adamant that I wasn't going back to Wisbech and in the end everyone involved acquiesced. This took a long time, during which period I had no schooling at all. Then to complicate matters (or rather in the event to simplify them) I developed impetigo, which made my isolation imperative.

By the time I had recovered Stationers had re-opened in Hornsey as so many pupils had drifted back to London, and by the autumn term of 1942 I was having a relatively normal grammar-school education.

The to-ings and fro-ings of my first three years of secondary education, however, had ruined any prospect of academic success, but, thanks to one 'dug out', a Mr Woolley, who read to us from the *Times* leader columns and who encouraged us to be adventurous in our choice of literature, I encountered many new authors who intrigued and excited me. My principal discovery was the writings of Voltaire which, but for Mr Woolley, I would never have dreamt of tackling.

2

The World of Work

By the time I was fifteen, in 1943, it was clear that apart from a sketchy acquaintance with literature and an ability to draw I was no scholar, and it was agreed that it would be better for everybody if I left school and went to work. A good friend of my brother, Den Berry, led a semi-professional dance band at night and worked as an arranger and copyist at the music publishers Laurence Wright by day. On his suggestion I applied for and got the job of office boy in a neighbouring publishers, Peter Maurice in Denmark Street, London's Tin Pan Alley.

I amused the hierarchy of Peter Maurice and they generated in me a new ambition. I now wanted to become a song plugger, a breed that is extinct today but whose job it was then, by cajoling and bribing singers, bandleaders and BBC producers, to get their company's songs on radio.

In those pre-television days a song broadcast regularly on radio would almost certainly become a best-seller, and rival publishers would go to extreme lengths to get their particular number into the repertoire of as many dance bands and crooners as possible.

A lot of money changed hands and the BBC producers who were concerned with these dance band and variety programmes were prime targets for the pluggers. As the average BBC producer in the 1940s earned around £600 a year it's easy to see how tempting a few hundred more from a friendly music publisher could be, and bribery and corruption flourished. As a fifteen-year-old would-be song plugger I was unaware of all this but realised that it was an industry where a lot of money could be made.

In those days most of the profit made by the music publishers was in sheet music which generally cost sixpence or a shilling a copy. At the time I joined Peter Maurice fetching tea, packing parcels, going to the post office, taking music scores to recording studios and at Christmas delivering the masses of expensive presents to the aforementioned singers, bandleaders and BBC producers, their best-seller was Paper Doll ('I'm gonna buy a paper doll that I can call my own, a dolly other fellers cannot steal'). Shortly after they capitalised on the 8th Army's commandeering of the Afrika Korps' favourite song, Lilli Marlene, published the English version and sold the sheet music by the million.

Although I was the firm's dogsbody I still hoped that one day when a vacancy occurred I would be made a song plugger, but meanwhile I had to get on with the job I was paid (£1.50 per week) to do. So I packed parcels of sheet music and took them to the post office and ran errands and fetched tea from one of the two restaurants in Denmark Street, the Suffolk Dairy and Julie's. The Suffolk Dairy was a fairly dire hole of a place where for a penny or twopence you could buy a piece of unspeakable bread pudding or a cup of nearly undrinkable tea.

Julie's was much better, run by the Italian Polledri family, the male members of which had been interned as undesirable aliens when Italy entered the war in 1940. Now Italy was out of it and the male Polledris could get back to their proper work creating terrazzo floors while sister Julie ran the café. My particular friend was Giovanni (Johnny) Polledri, some years older than me and very much more sophisticated. He would talk about his life in the internment camp and how things were in Soho in 1943–4, which is to say what kind of crooked deals were being hatched and who ran the black market.

Wartime London was made for dishonesty, theft, prostitution and vice of all kinds. The more trivial sorts of dishonesty were practised on gullible teenagers like me. One saxophone player of my acquaintance sold me a 'jewelled' watch that stopped going almost as soon as it was on my wrist. It was of course a piece of junk and the watch repairer I took it to wouldn't touch it. Johnny Polledri just sighed when I told him about it and continued instructing me in the ways of the world.

There was one aspect of London life in those war years of which I quickly became aware, and that was prostitution. American soldiers flooded the capital and sought their pleasures where they could find them. In an alleyway behind Denmark Street, down which I used to trundle my trolley-load of parcels to the Post Office, was a house used by at least three whores. Going to work early in the morning or leaving late I would see these women with American GIs either leaving or arriving. I suppose at night in the blackout their raddled features escaped the scrutiny of the horny GIs, and God knows what diseases known and unknown they bequeathed to their customers.

This aspect of sex horrified me, and the sheer nastiness of the sordid liaisons put me off extra-curricular sex for life. The idea of going to a prostitute seemed then, as it has ever since, to be unthinkable. Not that I have anything against prostitutes, who clearly supply a need. Quite recently I was accosted by a plump, motherly looking tart in Shepherd Market. I answered politely to her question 'Looking for a good time?' 'No thank you, madam. I've already had one.' At which she had the grace to titter.

I am in no sense a prude and wouldn't wish to persuade anyone to change his or her way of life, but back in 1943 just seeing those poor women, one whom had a face that was being eaten away by, I assume, syphilis, did the job of keeping me chaste more effectively than any quantity of pious sermons. Later when I was older I mixed in very raffish company and was a companion of, but was never tempted to emulate, the behaviour of the villains whose company I sought. I came of age amazingly untouched by the experiences of my teens. Even then I skirted danger by luck, or rather a naivety that miraculously saw me through various scrapes untouched.

Life in London during 1944 was complicated by the unscheduled arrival of the V1 buzz bombs and the V2 rockets, courtesy of Dr Werner von Braun, who later was to be so helpful to the Americans with their rocketry. Sensible adults were frightened to death at the prospect of these virtually unstoppable missiles. But at the age of sixteen the excitement of standing on a rooftop watching explosions mushroom up from distant suburbs and making a dash for cover when you heard the engine of a V1 cut out (the signal for it to explode shortly after) far outweighed any nervousness you might feel.

*

By 1944 I was bored with working nine to five packing music and got a job as a cinema projectionist in the Gaumont Palace Cinema in Wood Green. I enjoyed life there and, as we didn't start until midday and had a day and a half day (from 5 pm) off, the work wasn't onerous. I was able to concentrate on trumpet practice in the mornings and fell easily into the pattern of working when other more sober citizens weren't. Another of the young projectionists was, like me, an enthusiastic fan of the dance bands of the day, particularly Frank Weir's Orchestra. After work in the cinema we'd hie ourselves to his home and listen to the BBC late-night programmes of dance music.

The team of projectionists included a dour chief whose ambition was to manage a shoe shop and who spent most of his time in the staff rest room reading books on management and such material as was germane to selling shoes. Why he wanted to forsake the comparative peace of the projection booth for the hurly burly of the world of the bunion and hammer toe – of cherry blossom, dark tan, stick-a-soles, boot laces, blakies, and dubbin – I know not, but that was his aim in life.

His deputy was a wild-eyed Nordic-looking man who I assumed had been invalided out of the Army for insanity. I never liked to ask what his ambitions were.

Watching films five-and-a-half days a week I learned something of the technique of film-making but also became deeply aware of how awful many of the films were. The good ones I remember clearly still. There was *Dead of Night*, a collection of mildly scary stories with a memorable performance by Frederick Valk and another by Michael Redgrave as a ventriloquist taken over by his dummy. There was also an amusing cameo from Naunton Wayne and Basil Radford as Charters and Caldicott (two characters they'd created in the Hitchcock masterpiece *The Lady Vanishes*) and it was a film I never tired of watching. Another winner was *The Picture of Dorian Gray*, shot in black-and-white but with the portrait of the ugly disease-racked Dorian suddenly and shockingly in colour – a tour de force.

On Sundays we had a different programme altogether: generally some obscure melodrama or detective story, old films often close to disintegration on which a close eye had to be kept to prevent the film leaping off the projector and cascading over the projection-room floor. When that did happen, as it did not infrequently, the booth was a scene of wild disorder while the audience booed and stamped until we got the thing going again. Our greatest cock-up was to show two reels of a Disney feature-length cartoon film, *The Three Caballeros*, upside down and backwards. It was the chief projectionist's day off and the mad assistant was responsible for the error, but we all got a sound ticking-off from the cinema manager and later on a stiff reprimand from head office.

*

At about this time I fell in with a bunch of Wood Green villains. They were small-time black marketeers and, that wonderful catch-all phrase of small-time crooks, General Dealers. They frequented the cafés near Wood Green tube station and had between them a fairly mordant wit and a penchant for colourful nicknames. One was known as Fiery Jack, another as the Dagenham Tiger, and a third as Harry Craddock the Forger. Years later when I was appearing on a variety bill in St Leonards on Sea this same man, whose real name now escapes me, turned out to be the theatre manager. 'Good God,' I said when I saw him, 'Harry Craddock the Forger.' 'Don't say that here,' he hissed. 'I've gone straight.'

The most exotic of these minor ruffians was known as Jumbo, and though I don't know quite why we quickly became friends. I think he may have felt that this skinny youth from a middle-class background was so different from anyone he'd known before that I was a novelty. For my part I was quite happy to play Boswell to this strange, quirky, working-class Johnson. Uneducated he may have been, but his brain was keen.

Let me describe him. He was about six feet tall with a round face, its appeal somewhat lessened by a long razor scar from his right eye to his chin acquired in his street-fighting days. He'd been called up and served in the Army, deserted, been recaptured, deserted again and then found once more by the military police. After doing time in the glasshouse he was posted to the 1st Army and shipped out to North Africa in time to help mop up Rommel's Afrika Korps and take part in the invasion of Italy.

Before that could happen he trod on a landmine which unobligingly blew his leg off. Invalided out of the army he had become notorious in north London for his evil temper, heavy drinking and belligerence – if involved in a fight he'd use his wooden army-issue crutch to devastating effect. He'd calmed down a bit when I first met him, and he told me later that he assumed I came from a moneyed family and that he could con some of that money out of me. By the time he realised that I was as broke as everyone else he'd become quite attached to me and we became if not great friends then at least constant companions.

His language was flowery and, surprisingly, he swore very little. If someone annoyed him he'd say, leaning close so that whoever was at the receiving end would get a good look at his razor scar, 'You silly old daft' or 'You do vex me'. The words were simple but the menace was spine-chilling. His general conversation was laced with cockney rhyming slang. Thus the tube became the Oxo (Oxo cube – tube) or after a well-advertised motor oil, the Essolube. When things went well it was a cry of 'It's all Tiddley Bates', but where that comes from, or what it meant beyond a verbal thumbs up, I never discovered. He was without fear and would limp across any main road, however thick the traffic, with a cry of 'They won't run you over, they're not allowed to'.

My contribution to our friendship was to tell him about the books I was reading, mainly the novels of Evelyn Waugh and A.G. Macdonell, the Sherlock Holmes stories and the plays of Bernard Shaw. Towards the end of our relationship I lent him the half dozen books I most cherished. He sold them.

An interesting side-light to my consorting with the local toughs was that simultaneously I was consorting with the police. One, PC Jim Musgrove by name, was a saxophone player who ran a small dance band and entertained in pubs and clubs when not on duty. He'd joined the Metropolitan Police in the thirties as an alternative to unemployment, and we became friends when he bought dance band scores from Peter Maurice. Well, to be accurate he cadged dance band scores, but he was a pleasant companion and I spent several evenings in his company, in pubs where he sang a range of naughty songs including one which started: 'Last week when the day was fine and clear, I went for a swim off Brighton Pier ...' the rhymes of which if spoken or sung would have been extremely offensive. As it was, by a cunning musical sidestep the seemingly inevitable rhyme with luck, or hunt or rock was avoided.

He had another song about a tattooed lady, sung to the tune of Galway Bay, which included the lines: 'Down her back she has the hunt in all its glory, with horses, hounds and huntsmen all so gay, but alas the hunt will never find its quarry – the fox has gone to earth in Galway Bay.'

When I left the music publishers and was no use to Jim Musgrove, our friendship faded for, to be truthful, we had little in common.

Early attempts at trumpet-playing echoed round our neighbourhood and the endless practising of scales caused several neighbours to complain. During one practice session there was a knock at the door. I opened it and there on the doorstep loomed an extremely large police inspector.

He said, 'Are you the person who is playing the trumpet?'

I gulped and admitted that I was.

He beamed. 'I've just moved into this area and I play trumpet too,' he said. 'Perhaps we could play some duets.'

And that we did in the months that followed. He was a useful friend too. He'd say, 'Steer clear of Wood Green tonight, Barry, we're picking up some of those villains you knock about with.'

*

About this time I also became a sort of extra member of a large family living in Wood Green. I'd met one of the daughters while signing on at the Labour Exchange. She was a clerk there and I think she took pity on me, thinking that by introducing me to her family she was saving me from a life of debauchery and petty crime.

The mother was a good soul, amiable and hospitable, and I got to know the large and sprawling family quite well. There were several daughters, all of whom married in due course, a son who was something of a ne'er-do-well and a much younger son and daughter whom I came to know, but less well than their older brothers and sisters. They were a warm and loving family, a stark contrast to my own mother and father.

By the time I was seventeen their marriage was going through a bad patch. My mother, with number one son away from home in the Navy and number two son scarcely visible, though horribly audible at trumpet practice, had turned her irritations into a permanent catechism of criticism of my father. He didn't take her out, he was no company at home, his brooding bad temper was too much for her, and so on.

My father's reply was silence, his revenge to push away his evening meal untouched, and on rare occasions when my mother goaded him into it their mutual dislike flamed into a screaming row.

I think my mother enjoyed these scenes. At last she was the central figure in a dramatic situation. I suspect my father may have met and fallen for a younger and more attractive woman than the person who, by then, my mother had become, but his strict sense of morality prevented him from fulfilling any lust he may have experienced.

The fact of the matter was that he was a clever, industrious man saddled, as he saw it, with a family who didn't appreciate him. This was mainly because he rarely gave us a chance to see him as he really was, a warm, affectionate and amusing man.

He left home for work at 5.30 every weekday morning and didn't get home until around seven in the evening. I remember coming home early one morning after a night out as my father was getting ready to go to work. To my surprise he didn't tick me off but gave me a friendly grin and a warm 'good morning' and offered me a cup of tea. We shared the tea and chatted. That 5.30 am meeting was one of the only moments of rapport I'd had with him in seventeen years and it was so unusual I remember it vividly still, over forty-five years later.

In 1945 the war was over and soon my brother, who'd joined the Navy in 1944, came back home with tales of experiences as a radar mechanic in Mombasa, Ceylon and Rangoon. The A-Bombs dropped on Hiroshima and Nagasaki had saved him and many thousands of Allied service men from active service against the Japanese. He was demobbed in 1946 and in June of that year I was called up for National Service in the RAF.

3

Aircraftsman Took Entertains

During the war I had been deeply impressed by the heroic image of the RAF and found those tall men in blue, with their wings and insignia, their medal ribbons and their racy slang, extremely glamorous. I had fantasies of becoming a rear gunner in a Lancaster bomber and lapped up any stories told by RAF men of my brother's group when they were on leave.

In the event, when I was called up in 1946 and joined the RAF, I was and remained throughout my service a clerk, and an AC2 at that.

However, my trumpet saved me from the menial tasks to which my rank, or rather lack of rank, had theoretically condemned me, first at Yatesbury in Wiltshire where I did my square bashing and then at Kirkham near Blackpool where I went on a course to learn shorthand and typing (but didn't). Finally at RAF Records Office Gloucester I quickly established contact with the local RAF dance band and played for station dances, concerts and occasional competitions organised by *Melody Maker* magazine.

At Gloucester, where I was posted early in 1947 and where I remained until demob in 1949, I arrived just in time for one of the worst winters in living memory. In my memory – *the* worst. It was so cold for so long that fuel supplies ran out and the order came 'Keep warm regardless'.

This was interpreted by the more anarchistic of my fellow 'erks' as licence to tear the camp apart. The climax came when a particularly adventurous group stole the flagpole and chopped it up for firewood. This was something the Camp Commander would not tolerate, for although he turned a blind eye to the ablution huts, where every bit of timber had been removed leaving only the plumbing exposed to the sub-zero temperatures, he regarded removing the flagpole, where every morning the flag was ceremoniously raised and each evening lowered, as an act of vandalism.

After much recrimination and threats of mass punishment if the culprits did not own up the affair died down, non-essential personnel were sent home on indefinite leave and eventually spring came.

With spring the revitalised dance band started playing again and at its peak featured many first-class musicians. There was Peter McGurk, who after demob joined the Dudley Moore Trio, on bass, pianist Ossie Payne, who replaced an old schoolfriend of mine, Doug Pemberton, who was a sensational player but never turned pro, preferring the security of a regular job. Ossie, who as well as being an excellent pianist was a first-rate boxer, *did* turn pro when back in civvy street and was, when I last heard, leading his own band. Our guitarist was Tony Hayes who was later to be one of the founders, with Jimmy Fraser, of the Fraser Hayes Four who for many years graced the radio series *Beyond Our Ken* and *Round the Horne*. A man called Ron Simmonds played lead trumpet and went on to greater things in the dance band world, and our drummer, Ken Clare, was years later recognised as one of the best in the world and toured extensively with Tony Bennett. He died, sadly, some years ago of cancer. Peter McGurk committed suicide, and I have lost track of the others. Oh yes, the band leader, Peter Leeds, was an accordionist who held the group together. There were, of course, others – a trombonist who played out of the side of his mouth, and several excellent saxophone players. But, like grain and grape, saxophonists and brass players rarely mix.

It was Peter McGurk who introduced me to the girl who was to become my wife. Her name was Dot Bird, and she was a WAAF and a dance-band groupie. She was always at our dances, gyrating in the style of the time, a sort of watered down jitterbugging, with another girl called Ronnie. They (with others) manned the switchboard at the busy Records office, and I'd meet Dot after dances, walk back to her billet and after a chaste goodnight kiss head for my own quarters. My quarters I say, as if they were special. They weren't. I had a bunk and a bedspace in a hut containing thirty men. I ought to add, thirty of the most diverse types, both ethnically and in personality. There were men from Nigeria, the West Indies, Ireland, Scotland, Wales and all parts of England.

In 1948 came the Berlin Airlift and, as a clerk (who had done very little clerking), I was placed at a desk and took part in the exercise called at the time 'Remobilisation in the event of war'. This consisted of plans to recall ex-RAF personnel if the Berlin business looked like escalating.

But the 1948 flap was soon over, the Berlin Airlift continued and meanwhile there were hundreds of servicemen milling about Gloucester waiting to be demobbed and thirsting for entertainment.

The aircraftsman who ran the camp concert party, Howell Evans, returned to civvy street and I was asked to take over. I had for a long time been a regular theatregoer and shared with everyone who saw him a great admiration for Sid Field, the Midlands comedian who had been kept out of London's West End because of an unbreakable contract but who on its expiration became *the* major British comedy star of the 1940s. In *Strike a New Note, Strike It Again* and *Piccadilly Hayride* at the Prince of Wales theatre, Field had come to dominate completely the West End scene. Only the coming of the great American stars Danny Kaye, Jack Benny and Bob Hope showed that there were people as funny as Sid Field. There were other West End shows full of laughter too, and the music hall was booming. Enough material there for a light-fingered AC2 to filch and stage and put on presentable shows.

I called my friends together, found a splendid pianist in George Dobinson, who was also working out his national service as an RAF clerk, wrote some sketches, rehearsed furiously and eventually produced the first of many shows which delighted the uncritical RAF audience.

The show was called *It's a Pleasure* and was a mixture of songs, sketches and monologues. My second venture, *Nuts in May*, was better, the third, an attempt at a musical farce, was not so good and subsequently I reverted to the equivalent of music-hall bills until I too was demobilised. Although the material was fairly derivative the audience didn't know this and was vastly entertained.

I ventured into a double act with a fellow clerk, John Martindale, used an Irish tenor, also a great friend, Frank McDonnell, and co-opted any WAAF who was built like a regular human being. Costumes were obtained from West End costumiers thanks to a grant from the Air Ministry, and looking back I suppose we offered, by the standards of the day, reasonable entertainment. Better than that, our ace in the hole – a sure trump card in any show – was a handsome Welsh aircraftsman called Dai Francis. He was obsessed with Al Jolson and sang all his songs with the Jolson fervour. I thought it was corny, but the RAF audiences lapped it up. Later, national audiences lapped up the Dai Francis manner as he knocked them cold as one of the principals of *The Black and White Minstrel Show*. Dear Dai, how we used to mock him back at Gloucester in 1948 and oh, my, how wrong we were.

Another excellent performer came to us by chance. His name was Johnnie Reynolds and he had been in the RAF during the war. After being demobbed he became disenchanted with civilian life and re-enlisted in the RAF as an Aircraft Hand General Duties, or ACH GD, the lowliest in the Service. He was hoeing the CO's garden when his papers came through from the Air Ministry. It turned out (shades of my own failed ambition) that he'd been a Flight Sergeant, Air Gunner in Lancasters, had been wounded in action and had a silver plate in his skull, and had won the DSM (Distinguished Service Medal) for bravery, and there he was digging the CO's garden. As soon as the CO had digested the information received from the Air Ministry he ordered AC2 Reynolds into his office. Fifteen minutes later he emerged as Sergeant Reynolds with his appropriate medal ribbons and insignia sewn onto his tunic. A touch of humanity in the all-too-often earthbound RAF.

Another airman, a corporal, I got to know in the line of *his* duty, which was as NCO in charge of an ablution block. He wielded a mop with a certain élan but used to tell all his customers that he was counting the days to his demob. Eventually the day came and he departed. But three weeks later he was back wielding the same mop in the same ablution block, albeit now in civilian clothes. We asked him why he'd returned to his previous occupation. His answer was simple, 'I missed the old place.'

I left the RAF with few regrets. I'd not been much of an asset to them as an Aircraftsman, but as the CO said before I left, 'Thank you for entertaining these tough young airmen. To the others of your group I have suggested signing on. There's a career ahead in the RAF for a bright young man, but I feel your future is in entertainment. I hope you make it to the top.'

A footnote to my RAF career is that from the age of eighteen (to the present day) I have been incredibly clumsy. In addition to that, in my youth I was tall, skinny and bespectacled. (It was said of me, by the old crones of north London who muttered such things, 'He'll never make old bones.') When marching and counter-marching I was either the despair of or a source of amusement to drill sergeants who often invited their colleagues to watch this strange, gangling creature attempt to present arms without dropping his rifle and bayonet. If there was a parade or an inspection by some senior officer I was told by the NCO in charge 'Go and hide', and so I went through my entire time in the RAF without ever going on parade.

In the unlikely event of my ever having achieved the role of the rear gunner I'd dreamed of becoming I'd have probably shot the tail off the Lancaster bomber in which I was flying.

My clumsiness didn't extend to my stage performances, or rather I was able to harness it to good effect, and whether in drag singing 'There was I waiting at the Church', in an old-time music-hall routine, or indulging in a speciality of ours where a droll airman from Bristol, called Ron Gore, whom I'd recruited into our troupe, Johnnie Reynolds and I would, taking a section each, render a Danny Kaye routine from the film *Up in Arms*, suitably mangled for the delectation of the entertainment-hungry airmen of RAF Gloucester.

Going back to that part of Gloucestershire recently I found the old place gone; my brief RAF past wiped out. I was no dam-buster, but I survived.

4

Home and Away

Having set my sights on a career in show business I intended, when I was at last liberated from the RAF, to learn the business from the bottom up. I applied for and got the job of assistant electrician at the Wood Green Empire, a job which, though poorly paid, I came to enjoy enormously. The work wasn't terribly difficult. I ran the lighting switchboard during performances and helped with the theatre maintenance during the day. The senior members of the staff had many years of experience behind them and were full of anecdotes of showbusiness, all of which I lapped up. The excitement of a week in a variety theatre with new lighting plots, fresh cues and new people to cope with meant that, though not glamorous, life was never dull. Best of all, in twice nightly variety you saw the stars in all their glory twelve times from first house Monday until second house Saturday.

My favourites back in 1949 were Vic Oliver and Arthur Askey. Askey sprayed his jokes about stalls, circle and back stage, wanting to amuse everybody. In contrast Vic Oliver, when watched from the wings, didn't appear to be funny at all and yet you could hear the audience laughing. It was a curious phenomenon. One night I asked if I could go through the pass door and watch him from the back of the stalls. It was a fascinating experience. He was wry, witty, smutty in a sophisticated way, and very very funny. Where he differed from Askey was that he directed his work at his audience, those who had paid to sit in the stalls and circle, spurning the easy laughter that could be had from an admiring group of performers and stage hands in the wings. I'm not denigrating Askey, who was in his day a genuinely funny man, but Vic Oliver was a businessman. Laughter-making was his business and he wasn't going to squander it on anyone who didn't pay.

He was Viennese, and in World War One had served in the Austrian Army. He was basically a musician, played violin and piano well, but on going to America in the 1920s had switched to comedy. He came to Britain in the thirties, was taken up by society and married Winston Churchill's actress daughter Sarah.

It's interesting to speculate on what Churchill made of this Viennese Jew who was his son-in-law and who, while Churchill was spurring Britain to victory in World War Two, made his living by cracking risqué jokes in the music halls. Vic Oliver was also very successful in radio, particularly in company with two American movie stars, Bebe Daniels and Ben Lyon, who had come to Britain in the thirties, liked it and stayed.

In the forties and fifties a number of Hollywood stars came to Britain, including Carmen Miranda, Red Skelton and Laurel and Hardy, but one of the strangest visitors to the music-hall circuit was Peter Lorre. One didn't expect the weasely Joel Cairo from *The Maltese Falcon* to crack gags on the stage of a north London variety house. But there he was at the Wood Green Empire, as a part of his tour of Britain, in a comedy sketch with an English actress. More in keeping with his persona as something creepy from the movies, in the second part of the programme he declaimed the Edgar Allen Poe monologue, 'The Tell Tale Heart'.

It's about a murderer suffering the tortures of conscience as he seems to hear his victim's heart still beating. My part of the action, as the switchboard operator, was gradually to dim the lights and at the crucial moment blackout. Very theatrical and very effective it was, and the audience loved the piece. I should mention that my post was on a platform several yards high and to one side of the stage. There I stood in lonely state with the knobs and handles of the antiquated lighting board mine to command. On Saturday nights, after the last performance, I shut everything down, shinned down the ladder and went home.

At the end of Peter Lorre's week I went through my routine

and was walking across the darkened stage when Lorre appeared out of the shadows and hissed at me. I was so startled I jumped like a scalded cat. But as it turned out he only wanted to thank me for my efforts at lighting him, and pressed a pound note into my hand. Not only that, but we chatted for ten minutes, Lorre telling me how much he'd come to love England and the English. Far from being the sinister monster he so often portrayed on the cinema screen, Peter Lorre was a generous and amusing man.

Among the lesser-known acts playing the halls in those days were some delightful old-stagers such as Dickie Henderson Senior, whose only bow in the direction of stage make-up and props was to put a blob of red on the end of his nose, stick a grey bowler at a rakish angle on his head and dance lightly out on stage singing 'Tiptoe Through the Tulips'. As he was rather fat, with a protruding stomach, the effect was bizarre, to say the least. Then there was a balancing act, a father and son whose stage name I now forget, who as a climax would balance head to head (the son upside down) and play piano accordions. It wasn't that which made it so memorable but the father's muttered asides, such as 'I'm chucking this game when I'm twenty three', and 'Ah, well, seven years soon slip away'. The ludicrous inappropriateness of things like that have stayed with me ever since, typical of the whimsical surrealism of the day, the stock-in-trade of some of those lovable bygone entertainers.

*

Though things were going swimmingly at the Wood Green Empire, I was itching to move. I'd developed an act of sorts and wanted to try it out at the various pubs and working-men's clubs that paid small sums of money to up-and-coming entertainers, a pound a performance being about average. John Martindale and I had tried a double act at these same clubs when we were first demobbed, but it didn't work and John wisely went from there into advertising, becoming in due course one of the top men in the British end of the Wrigley's Chewing Gum empire.

I left the Wood Green Empire with many a grim warning about the precariousness of music-hall life and the suggestion that if I was wise I'd stick with them where the pay, if not spectacular, was at least regular. In fact it was disgracefully low, for when the top of the bill could easily earn several hundred pounds a week a stage hand would, for a long week's work, get something less than five pounds.

Obviously I needed to get a day job, and I decided to go back to music publishing. I got a job at Paxtons Music Co. as their export clerk, which meant assembling large amounts of sheet music, teaching manuals and the collected essays of music teachers and critics for despatch to South Africa, Australia and New Zealand. These included, and I bless the publishers (Constable) for reprinting his work, Bernard Shaw, whose collected music criticisms I found the most stimulating reading imaginable.

Browsing through the music files at Paxtons I found several forgotten gems of song which I started to use in my act. For, as I'd hoped, once or twice a week I'd be booked to appear at a working men's club in Dagenham or Lambeth, Camberwell or Neasden.

I cracked a few jokes, played trumpet and finished with a song. With the trumpet I 'borrowed' an idea I'd seen in an American film and used a glove puppet which, with the middle finger of my right hand operating the head and my index and third fingers working the arms, I could play such gems as 'The Teddy Bears' Picnic'. It was moderately novel, people liked it and I became quite popular in the limited field of working men's clubs and, when really uninhibited, could make a roomful of uncritical cockneys and their wives laugh their heads off. In fact at the Lambeth Liberal Club I became quite a local hero.

Meanwhile my personal life changed somewhat. In August 1950 Dot and I were married at the Wood Green Register Office and went to live in a flat in Church Crescent, Muswell Hill, which we shared with my brother and his wife Pearl, who had married a few months before. The flat comprised four large rooms, so each couple had a living room and a bedroom and we shared a large kitchen, the bathroom facilities and a garden.

The house backed onto a one-track railway line (long since defunct). A few carriages were pulled by a steam engine that chugged noisily from Alexandra Palace to Highgate where one changed for the Northern Line.

Where we lived you could hear it coming, and a brisk dash down the road would get you to the local station as the train drew in. It was a remarkable sight to see the entire male population of the Crescent come out of their front doors like so many greyhounds out of their traps and pelt down the road, neck and neck, to catch that train.

Looking back it seems fun, but wasn't that funny at the time as we were all as poor as church mice. Dot and I had a joint income of about ten pounds a week plus what I earned in the clubs. My brother, now having graduated from London University with a BSc and starting on his career as a physicist, earned somewhat more, and Pearl, an artist, supplemented what her paintings and drawings brought in with occasional forays into temporary work of one kind or another. On the whole the domestic arrangement worked out well and we only had the occasional dispute. I no longer made my brother laugh as I had when we were children, but he was quietly confident that I could make it as a professional comedian. In fact he thought I could do better than that and persuaded me to take an acting course at night school.

The classes were held at Toynbee Hall in London's East End, a cultural oasis in those days. We met, a group of fifteen or so of us, each Tuesday and Thursday evening and were taught the rudiments of acting, mime and improvisation by a talented team of teachers from the Old Vic School.

One student in our class was outstanding both physically and in talent, and our tutors moved whatever theatrical mountain was necessary to get him accepted as a full-time student at the Old Vic. His name was Bernard Bresslaw and he more than lived up to everyone's expectations by becoming a television star in Granada's *The Army Game*, and a regular in Peter Rogers's *Carry On* films.

Others in our group were Edward Caddick, who became an actor and writer, and Jane Higgins, a physiotherapist, with whom I developed a great rapport. It was, I regret to say looking back, entirely platonic, but we went to the theatre and opera together, visited art galleries and talked endlessly about politics, religion and the stage.

I really enjoyed those evening classes at Toynbee Hall. The group I was with were stimulating, ambitious and fun. Our tutors were excellent and taught us the basics of the Old Vic method based largely on the works of the great Russian teacher Stanislavski.

First: relaxation – surprisingly difficult to master but crucial to any actor seeking to achieve repose. Then improvisation which, when it works, is like falling lightly through space and making a gentle landing. We'd be told things like 'You're a husband visiting his wife in hospital, and Ted is the doctor whose job it is to tell you she died on the operating table.' Or, 'You and Jane are lovers on a park bench, and Bernard is the park keeper.' Simple themes but they produced a lot of good, imaginative work.

Mime always left me cold, for although (like everyone who has ever seen him) I can give impressions of Marcel Marceau walking against the wind or leaning on the mantelpiece, I never felt drawn to that particular discipline.

We tackled one production in our first year. Thornton Wilder's *Our Town*, a fascinating piece telling the story of life in a small American town with the stage manager as narrator. Thanks to my experience, limited though it was, as a stand-up comic I was cast as the stage manager.

All these acting experiences broadened my mind and showed me glimpses of a life I might aspire to.

*

At home, however, things were not going too well. It had become obvious to me after only a few months that getting married had been a terrible mistake, but Dot was now pregnant and although we had little in common the baby on the way prevented me from any other course but that of staying put and building the best life I could for both – rather, the soon to be three – of us.

Life in Church Crescent was far from dull. Classmates from Toynbee Hall were frequent visitors, Philip and Pearl had made many friends in their university days and the flat was full of people chatting, playing bridge, devising as well as solving crossword puzzles or acting in complicated charades.

Our next-door neighbours in Church Crescent were two families who shared the house, Peggy and Francis Apprahamian, and Roy and Dorothea Zemla. Three were school teachers: Francis, the odd one out, was a research assistant to Professor Bernal at London University. They were all members of the Communist Party and among the nicest people I've ever known.

Their politics, let me add, fell somewhere between Bernard Shaw and Mikhail Gorbachev, and in the early fifties being a Communist was still OK, as whatever the internal horrors of the USSR, people still remembered that the German Army had been broken at Stalingrad, Leningrad and Kiev and finally destroyed by the Red Army in the rubble of Berlin.

My best friend of our quartet of Communist neighbours was Roy Zemla, who was wonderfully helpful in many ways and had great understanding of my marital problems. In the late 50s we went to Paris together, staying with a French Communist party member and meeting a number of journalists and left-wing intellectuals.

Roy thought it would be an amusing idea to pass me off as the illegitimate brother of Lord Snowdon, who was about to marry Princess Margaret. Our Communist journalist friends who were writing for *Canard Enchainé* and *La Parisienne*, which had readerships besotted by gossip concerning the Royal Family, fell for the wheeze hook, line and sinker, and Roy and I fabricated tales of great variety and ingenuity of lust and indiscretion in London's High Society. When we finally owned up and told them we were kidding they were most disappointed but I suspect printed our inventions as 'exclusives' later.

Roy had studied at the Sorbonne and, being a Jew, had grown up in the anti-Nazi left-wing atmosphere of pre-war and wartime Europe. His wife, Dorothea, was a pragmatic and fairly unemotional woman, whereas Roy loved laughter and convivial company. It was in their home that I met some of the real French Resistance fighters, tough railwaymen from Strasbourg and Metz who recounted with immense glee tales of wartime sabotage; derailing German supply trains, blowing up ammunition dumps and creating endless delays in order to help the Allied forces during the Normandy invasion in 1944. Had any of their comrades been shot by the Nazis? They shrugged: 'Yes, many. But we were at war. Casualties were inevitable.' Not *'Allo 'Allo* but something much better. These were brave men fighting for their country and their beliefs.

Peggy Apprahamiam was more romantic than the others. She ran a troop of 'The Woodcraft Folk', a pacifist alternative to the Scouts and Guides. I have no doubt it was a subversive movement, as any group who prefer peace to war must be, but pacifists are by their very nature harmless people and no threat to anyone.

Francis bounced with life and vigour, forever cracking jokes and organising outings and meetings and taking his turn with the rest of the Muswell Hill members of the CP, all of them bright and gifted, and most of them Jews, in selling the *Daily Worker* at street corners on Saturday mornings. His brother, Felix, was for many years the music critic of the *Sunday Times*.

Having left school at fifteen and worked from the beginning in the 'free market' economy of music publishing and entertaining, Communism never appealed to me as more than a splendid theory that didn't seem to work in reality. That the Russians, who had suffered terrible casualties during the war, were brave and resilient there was no doubt. British Government propaganda during the war had extolled the virtues of 'our Russian Comrades', and the tyrant Stalin was affectionately known as 'Uncle Joe'. Still, I felt that Communism wouldn't work in Muswell Hill, which seemed stable and comfortable and not ripe for revolution.

I must admit that the philosophy of 'give what you are able and take what you need' has always seemed a slogan that one could live by and echoes the old Christian prayer, 'Let me be neither rich nor poor.'

A society motivated by greed has never appealed to me, and the Zemlas and the Apprahamiams were anything but greedy: to my mind at any rate, entirely splendid.

5

Show Biz!

Howell Evans, whose successor I'd been, running the Concert Party at RAF Gloucester, was, in 1951, compèring a Good Friday concert for Carroll Levis, the Canadian talent spotter, at the Granville Theatre, Walham Green, something of a fleapit and definitely down-market. Short of talent, he invited me to take part, and I agreed. The audience were rowdy, and the poor comic who went on just ahead of me was booed and catcalled and showered with pennies. Then a tiny girl sang 'We'll Gather Lilacs' in a trembling soprano, and it was my turn.

My experience in the working men's clubs stood me in good stead and I battled with the audience, won them over and made my exit to cheers. So impressed was Howell Evans that he arranged for me to meet the great Carroll Levis himself, who shortly after was appearing for the week at the Brixton Empress. I duly met Levis, to be greeted with 'You're the guy that they threw pennies at at the Granville.' I assured him I wasn't, and rather grumpily he arranged for me to be included as part of the show the following Friday.

Shaking with nerves I duly appeared, and although I wasn't pelted I was not terribly impressive. Nor was Levis terribly impressed, but comedians of any kind were hard to come by and a few weeks later he gave me another chance and let me go on again when his Company were playing the Chelsea Palace. On the face of it there was not much difference between the audience at Brixton and the one at Chelsea but, now more used to the environment and, thanks to Toynbee Hall, more confident, I went on and did well. So much so that Levis, never given to much praise, said when I came off: 'Why the hell didn't you do that at Brixton?' Anyway, the following week the show was at Shepherd's Bush and Levis put me on for the whole week. Not only that but he paid me twelve pounds. That plus the day job meant I'd earned more in one week than ever before. Little did I know that it would be several years before I earned much more. But, although only *semi*-professional, I was now in show-business.

On the Sunday following our week at Shepherd's Bush was the first of the Levis radio talent contests in which I was scheduled to appear. I did and won my way into the final with comparative ease.

The next week we were at Chiswick Empire and then Hackney Empire and I was preparing my act for the final of the Radio Talent Contest. Not being too sure of my material I had asked the BBC producer about possible script writers. He suggested Bob Monkhouse, who was even then, in 1951, a well-known broadcaster and scriptwriter. As coincidence would have it I'd met Bob in the Charing Cross Road branch of Cecil Gee, the 'with it' menswear shop of the day, shortly after I was demobbed. We were both buying civvy clothes (Bob had been demobbed at the same time as me) and, clothes being rationed, had been given clothing coupons with which to equip ourselves for civilian life.

As it happened Bob had left his coupons at home. I lent him some of mine, and he returned them later at a Soho coffee bar, where he introduced me to his partner, Denis Goodwin. They were well-established, I had yet to begin, but eighteen months later I found myself on the threshold of a career without material. Bob had by then a stable of writers, and one of these, Eric Merriman, was deputed to help me out.

He made some suggestions, offered a tip or two, gave me some gags and, I think, sent me a bill for £5 for the job. As that was my fee for appearing I had early warning that (a) it was more profitable to write than perform, and (b) if I did radio for nothing it might enhance my career but it would do nothing for my income.

The man tipped to win the 1951 Carroll Levis talent contest was a West Indian singer of romantic songs, 'Lucky' Robinson.

He was very good and we got on well, but it turned out that he was less than lucky for in the final he faltered a little, and the partisan London audience made it clear that I was their favourite.

It seems incredible looking back that a radio show in the early 1950s could attract an audience in the region of twenty million, but that's what the Levis series got and I received hundreds of letters of congratulations from friends, relatives and complete strangers, including one from a clergyman inviting me to stay with him in his vicarage in North Wales, telling me he was single but, to quote him, 'I'm as human as the next man'. It was quite obvious that the poor old soul was as queer as a clockwork banana and I must have sounded to his fevered imagination as possibly a kindred spirit. Well, I wasn't and I replied politely by post that unfortunately I was unable to accept his kind offer. Other letters were more interesting, coming from old RAF colleagues, some of the Toynbee Hall gang, and more cousins than I believed I had.

Thanks to my success on the air, Levis offered to take me on on a permanent basis. I leapt at the chance, gave my notice to Paxtons and at the end of August 1951 started on my professional career.

Our first out-of-town date was in Manchester at the Hulme Hippodrome. The Levis show did well during its week and I had my first taste of theatrical digs, the lodging houses famed in many a scurrilous anecdote circulated by the theatrical profession. I can remember a week in Rochdale in digs so foul that no caring person would have kept an animal there.

On another occasion I paid fifteen shillings for a week in a bed-sitting room in Derby. Admittedly I supplied the food, but the landlady cooked it. I think that was probably the best value for money I ever had. But during that first week as a 'pro' in Manchester I was too taken up with the novelty of being on tour and in a city I'd only visited briefly once before, when in the RAF, to hear the Hallé Orchestra, to worry about the damp bed and awful food of my digs and, in fact, went through the week in a kind of daze.

By the Saturday of that first week on tour I'd settled sufficiently to fancy going to a football match, and wandering out into the street asked a passer-by the way to the football stadium.

'Which one?' he asked, 'United or City?'

'Which one is best?' I asked.

He looked at me as if I was crackers. 'I support United,' he said.

'Well, that'll do me then,' I said.

'But they're playing away,' he said.

'Oh, well then I'll try City.'

And even though he was a Manchester United supporter he kindly walked with me to the City ground, chatting of this and that.

Before he left to go about his business he said, 'You're not from round here are you?'

I admitted I wasn't.

'Nay, I thought not,' he said, and walked briskly off.

I went to see Manchester City play and have enjoyed watching them ever since.

On stage I was doing my best, but I wasn't getting the laughs I'd got in London. At Leeds it was a little better, but at Blackpool I wasn't received well and I think there was a strong possibility that, if I hadn't gone a great deal better the following week in Morecambe at the Winter Gardens, I'd have been sacked.

If Levis could pass his discoveries off as 'local boys (or girls) making good' he did. But some of his regulars were hard-bitten and experienced, having toured with him for some years. These characters, generally instrumentalists (xylophone, harmonica or trumpet players – rare birds at auditions) were known to us colloquially as 'the old lags', and it's not that easy to describe a gnarled harmonica player or clearly middle-aged comedian as a local newcomer. However, whenever we played in London (Finsbury Park, Shepherd's Bush or Chiswick Empires) I'd be introduced as coming from Finsbury Park or Chiswick, or Shepherd's Bush. Levis also delighted in creating 'Bill Matter', the description of the act under the name of the artiste. At one time I was called the Lanky Londoner, and on another occasion London's Longest Laugh, though generally it was Barry Took The Lanky Look.

Other examples of the Levis touch in bill matter were 'Eddie

Wood – He's always good' and 'Dave Gray – Laughingly Gay'. Both were north-country comedians, excellent in their way, who in the soft atmosphere generated by the assumption of the amateur status of us 'discoveries' got good reactions from the audience, but 'Laughingly Gay'?!

Billing for singers sometimes baffled Levis, 'Glasgow's Lovely Soprano' being about the best he could manage; but he excelled himself with the billing for one lad whom, I think, he had picked up in an audition in Cardiff, by describing him as 'Manny Barboza, Latin America's Troubador – First Time in England', which assuming his Welsh ancestry may well have been true.

Levis, an ex-Montreal policeman, had come to the UK in 1935 to make his fortune and, with regular radio coverage both with the BBC and Radio Normandie, on the Quaker Oats programme, he quickly made a name and a fortune. He made a few stars, and some time before I met him he had had a serious breakdown and had been in an institution. His brother, Cyril, soldiered on for a while but the old magic wasn't there and when Carroll was fit again Cyril returned to Canada and Carroll went back on the road.

When I auditioned for him, Carroll Levis was making a comeback and although supposed not to drink had often had quite a skinful when he came on stage. In those moods he could be fairly sadistic. The routine as far as I was concerned was that he'd introduce me (e.g. – 'A big welcome to a local boy – Lewisham's Lanky Lunatic'), we'd chat for a minute or two, he'd pat me on the back and depart, commanding the audience to give me 'a big hand'. I'd then go into my act. When drunk, his pats on the back became vicious slaps that really hurt. One night he was in a particularly bad mood and he was about to give what I could see was going to be a haymaker. He swung his arm – I dodged and his momentum spun him round and landed him in the orchestra pit.

After that there were no pats on the back and, in fact, shortly afterwards he gave up drinking for good, much to the relief of all concerned.

My act? I told a few gags and sang a song, generally 'How could you believe me when I said I loved you when you know I've been a liar all my life' (a title only slightly shorter than the song itself). Later I invented a routine based on the coming of cinemascope, the wide-screen innovation of the day. Most of the early cinemascope films seemed to be set in ancient Rome and I seized on this for my parody.

I'd go to one side of the stage, put on a prop toga and call, 'Oh, mighty Caesar – I bring you news from Rome.' I would then run as fast as I could across the stage to the other proscenium arch and, as Caesar with a laurel wreath on my head, say 'What news, messenger?' Then I'd rush back to the other side and cupping my hand to my ear say 'What?' I'd then run back and ask the question again, and so on ... It was an amazingly successful routine; so much so that it was appropriated by, among other people, Jim Dale and Tommy Cooper!

*

On 29 September 1951 I was delighted to get the news that I'd become a father. There had been no problems for Dot, and the baby was a boy whom we named Barry Christian. Levis announced on stage the fact that I'd become a father that day and the audience duly applauded. He commented, 'Why are you applauding *him* – his wife did all the work!'

If a child had come into my life that week, love had certainly come into Levis's. As one of the judges of the Miss Britain beauty contest he naturally took an interest in the winner, inviting her on stage that night to take a bow. The winner's name was Violet Pretty and indeed she was a striking-looking girl, a bit gauche perhaps but certainly a looker. Levis, who had always been susceptible to ladies' charms, fell for her heavily. (Violet Pretty – her real name incidentally – subsequently became a film star under the name of Anne Heywood and appeared in many films.)

Levis, a large, portly man with a fleshy, open face and a lot of energy but with startlingly white hair for a man in early middle age, was very attractive to women. His opening gambit, 'Do you believe in love the first night?', was fairly unsubtle but obviously touched a chord in those repressed provincial middle-class ladies who seemed to find in Levis their ideal lover.

Indeed ideal he must have been: famous, wealthy, a man of the world, and never around for too long!

His wife, Mina, was a bright, intelligent woman who, I guess, had settled for the Park Lane penthouse where they lived: money, clothes and a quiet life, turning a blind eye to his philandering. On first seeing her at one of the radio shows, looking stunning, and assuming that she was another Levis hanger-on, I said to Carroll 'Who is that marvellous-looking lady?' and received the time-honoured reply – 'That's no lady, that's my wife.' I don't think Levis was aware that he'd cracked the oldest joke in the business.

But Mina had what so few of his one-night stands possessed – class. Violet Pretty though was no one-night stand, and shortly after they met he installed her in a Piccadilly apartment. What's more he took her on tour with him. About this time he decided to put another company of discoveries on the road. We tried out at a theatre in Aldershot and to my surprise I was asked to compère and (in theory) manage this second company. I say in theory because Levis's road manager, whom I won't name as he was subsequently sacked for fiddling the National Insurance contributions, actually came down, collected the profit on the week and paid the cast. In addition to the hour or so of regular discoveries there were five professional acts in the first half of the bill. Business was good and Levis decided, after discussion with his agent, Joe Collins (father of Joan, Jackie and the lesser-known Bill and Natasha) to make this second company a regular feature, with one professional act to start the show, then me introducing the old lags and after the interval Violet Pretty as compère introducing the youngsters of the company. I was also manager of the company and after a shaky start coped moderately well.

Business flourished, so much so that Violet Pretty took a company to the medium-range theatres while Carroll Levis played the No 1's and I did the rest: the creaking rat-infested horrors of the No 3 circuit. I was back to being king of the damned. I christened my show *The Show Stoppers* and relied heavily on local talent gleaned from auditions in every town we visited.

After a while I developed the knack of spotting performers who would be good on the air and recommending them to the boss. It must be admitted, however, that the standard of talent varied. On one occasion, in Tonypandy, I was faced by eight large male-voice choirs and dozens of excellent solo singers. That week we were deluged with talent. On another occasion, in Llanelli, the only people to turn up were a boy soprano, a ham-fisted juggler and an almost totally tone-deaf contralto. We got through the week somehow, but it was touch and go.

Other towns brought other surprises. Proud fathers would bring three-year-olds to lisp the latest pop songs, contortionists would get locked in bizarre poses, performing animals would get stage fright. One comedian's gimmick was that at the pay-off of a joke his glass eye would light up. He'd installed a small bulb in the eye and operated it from a battery in his trouser pocket. What made that particular audition so gruesome was that the comic took me to a dark corner of the theatre to demonstrate and, of course, when he pressed the switch not only was the glass eye illuminated but half his skull as well. It was one of the most unnerving experiences I've ever had.

Carroll Levis developed the habit of sending the trouble-makers of his company to me, often with the terse remark 'I'm sending you so and so. Let him play the week, then sack him.' I'd frequently make a plea for a stay of execution for these unfortunates who were, generally speaking, more talented than tactful. One, subsequently a successful radio disc jockey under the name of Tony Brandon, was in those days an impressionist and off stage was too ebullient for Levis. I managed to hang on to him. Tony and I are friends today, forty years on.

The good and the useful and the broadcastable generally got their break under the wishful catch-all phrase 'The discoveries of today are truly the stars of tomorrow', and though few made it (Jim Dale is the only star to have come from the Levis empire) many at least got a break.

Then there were the Sunday concerts where during the summer, at various coastal resorts, Levis could make a killing with an inexpensive troupe. Generally we'd rendezvous in London and travel by coach to the resort, for instance Clacton or Folkestone, play two performances and return to London.

One morning on the coach I sat, as I usually did, reading the Sunday papers. 'What's that you're reading?' said Levis. I told him, 'It's the *Observer*.' He said, 'The *Observer*? What are you, some kind of Communist?'

You can imagine that because I was away from home so much my marriage had not flourished during this period, but seeing Dot only briefly on rare occasions at least postponed the inevitable break-up for a while. Though not completely saintlike during my absences I never went beyond 'dalliance' and no landlady's daughter lost her virginity through me.

I think one anecdote reveals much about both Levis's and my attitude at that time. After each evening's performance I'd have to phone him to say how much we'd taken at the box office, how the show was being received and what, if anything, new in the way of talent had turned up at the auditions.

After one particularly successful week, at Blythe in Northumberland, the show was re-booked two weeks later and one of the local singers, a sweet-voiced girl by the name of June Barry (her husband was her accompanist and together they shone) suggested that by way of a change for our second week she should sing duets with her mother.

I thought it worth a try and put them on. They were terrific, brought the house down and would be clearly excellent for radio. When I reported this to Levis he said, angrily, 'But a mother? I don't want old ladies on the show – I want youth and energy.' I stuck to my point that as we were a family show nothing could be more suitable than a mother-and-daughter act. At least it was original and, besides, they were enormously talented. He grumpily agreed to give them a try out in one of the shows he presented, was as enthusiastic as I was once he'd heard them sing and, more to the point, heard the deafening applause they generated.

From then on they toured, with considerable success, with the Great Man on the No 1 circuit. When the mother finally decided it was time to retire she introduced her two other daughters to the show and, as The Barry Sisters, they prospered both with Levis and later on their own. I even sang with them on radio – a ghastly number called 'Sh-Boom'. As a thank-you the publisher put my picture on the cover of the sheet music, and it still turns up from time to time to haunt me as people find ancient copies and send them to me with tongue-in-cheek notes.

Many years later Noel Edmonds, having been sent a copy by a

young viewer of *Multi Coloured Swap Shop*, on which I was appearing, set me up and with piano accompaniment supplied by one of the production team insisted that I sing the song there and then live on television.

I struggled through it somehow and finished with a stage fall so realistic that Edmonds really thought I'd fainted with shock!

Back in my Levis days I was grateful for any boost to my career.

Little of interest occurred during my time with *The Show Stoppers*, except that on arrival at Barnsley on one tour I found that I'd developed mumps – extremely painful to an adult, and after some weeks out of action I returned to the main Levis troupe, doing a solo comedy routine.

I did go back to the managing/compèring treadmill for a while, but I was really itching to try my luck as a stand-up comic in my own right not buttressed by being a 'discovery'. So I duly left Levis and swam off into the sargasso sea of variety.

*

I must say, looking back, that I liked Carroll Levis. He was arrogant, something of a con man, a bit of a bully and certainly an amorous adventurer, but under his flamboyant exterior I think he was a sensible and caring man and I'm sure he liked and trusted me. I was certainly honest with him and feel no shame at having been at one time a Carroll Levis discovery.

Years later I ran into him in Bond Street. He'd not been doing well and his once distinctive white hair had been dyed black. He was trying to promote some new version of the Discoveries, without success, and looked down-at-heel and furtive. We exchanged a few words and parted, never to meet again, as some months later he died. He wasn't everybody's cup of tea, but he never hampered talent and was happy when occasionally one of his geese magically turned out to be a swan.

6

Going Solo

There is in the world of entertainment a beautifully frustrating Catch 22. (Catch 22, if you remember Joseph Heller's book about the US Airforce in Italy in World War Two, was one where if you were insane you would be sent home, but if you were sane enough to say you were insane you weren't insane enough to go home.)

In my early days it worked like this:

Would-be Comedian:	Will you represent me?
Agent:	Certainly, if I like your act. Where can I see you work?
Would-be Comedian:	Well, nobody will book me until I get an agent.
Agent:	Well, I can't book you until I've seen you work.
Would-be Comedian:	But if you can't see me work how can you book me?

and so on.

There were two ways out of that impasse. One was to audition for the Windmill Theatre where over the years Vivian Van Damm booked a number of up-and-coming comedians, Tony Hancock, Dick Emery and Jimmy Edwards among them, to enliven his nude revues which, with the proud title 'We never closed', catered for the dirty mac brigade for many years until the permissive society of the 1960s caught up with him and one could see much more explicit sex on tv and in the cinema than you could at his tiny theatre in Windmill Street. I auditioned for Van Damm when newly out of the Forces and was told, 'Come back when you have more experience.'

The other possible way of having your work seen was by appearing at the Nuffield Centre, a club for servicemen run by two excellent ladies, Mary Cook and Mary Forbes. I'd done little spots for the two Marys during my pre-Levis pub-and-club adventures and they'd been most encouraging, possibly more than I deserved; but they showed interest in me, as did another of their group, Freddie Ross, who many years later became the second Mrs Tony Hancock.

Shortly after I'd left Levis they held a showcase evening where agents, managers and radio and tv producers could have a look at the latest crop of talent. There were several acts on that bill apart from me, but I only remember three young lads who played and sang, were fresh-faced and talented. They were The King Brothers, and that evening at the Nuffield Centre set them on their way to success. Dennis King is now a successful composer, arranger and bandleader, but his two brothers have somewhat drifted from view.

It was pretty good for me too as I met and have worked for, on and off all through my life, one Dennis Main Wilson, a BBC producer. Dennis is a hard worker, a hard drinker and a great talent-spotter – and that night he spotted me. Also in the audience were Sonny Zahl, one of the group of agents working for Harry Foster in the old-established Fosters Agency, and Stanley Dale, one of the directors of Associated London Scripts and agent to many excellent performers, notably Frankie Howerd. He frequently put variety bills on at various music halls and was a useful, not to say important, man to know.

The outcome of the evening was that I signed a contract with Fosters Agency that guaranteed me £600 per year. Sonny Zahl became my agent; Stanley – known by most people as 'Scruffy' Dale – promised to book me on his variety bills; and Dennis Main Wilson offered me a job as general-purpose voice man in a radio series he was involved with called *Pertwee's Progress* starring Jon Pertwee, Fenella Fielding and Dick Emery, and written by Jimmy Grafton and Larry Stephens.

My job was to play any odd characters that happened to turn up in the script, my first being an effete whale (an effect produced by speaking into a loud-hailer placed on a bass drum). My epic line was 'Hello sailor – new in town?'

My first solo variety date was at the Kingston Empire on a bill put together by Stanley Dale which featured Billy Anthony, whose recording of 'This Old House' had recently made the charts, Tony Brent, a singer of sentimental ballads, some dancers, a juggler, Bruce Forsyth, acrobatic comedians Hope and Keen, and me. A number of bookers came to see Bruce Forsyth, who was full of energy, funny and very well received by the locals, and I'm sure that appearance at Kingston led directly to his stardom. For me it was good to be working on my own, and other dates soon followed.

In the 1950s the life of a music-hall artist, particularly a stand-up comedian, was not all laughter and applause. For a start, the music halls were in decline, killed finally by television but also dying of their own incompetence.

The well-established acts like Robb Wilton, Elsie and Doris Waters, Jimmy James and Donald Peers would do good business and gave the illusion that there was life still in the old dog variety. Of the newcomers Max Bygraves and Frankie Howerd, and later Morecambe and Wise, Ken Dodd and Des O'Connor could also fill theatres, but there were many alleged stars who had no pulling power, and all too many supporting acts who were either over the hill or just plain inept. Pantomimes still flourished, and indeed do today, but attempts to revive the music hall have failed, except for the Players Theatre whose old-time evenings hark back to an earlier age when the music halls were the only source of entertainment for the poor, and talent was brilliant and abundant.

At their peak, 1890–1920, the music-hall entertainers spoke, or more often sang, to their audiences about the things the audience knew and understood, from the scathing 'Burlington Bertie' with its ironic description of poverty, to the sentimental 'My Old Dutch' – 'We've been together now for forty years, and it don't seem a day too much ...' Those songs meant something to the music-hall audience.

Once that connection between performer and audience was picked up by the wireless and the cinema in the twenties and thirties, the old music halls were doomed. The arrival of television killed them forever.

*

Life for the touring comedian in the 1950s was pretty bleak. In one boarding house in Darlington I became convinced that rats were gnawing the floorboards and moved to more salubrious digs after one sleepless night.

In Blackburn I remember the landlady was so impressed at seeing me in a dinner jacket and compèring the show in a 'BBC accent' that she told me she thought I was too sophisticated to drink tea and invested in a tin of Nescafé (she pronounced it Nestlecaff) which she served at breakfast, tea and supper.

Digs varied in quality. In one northern town I was asked if I would 'share' with another solo act. The share meant sharing the same bed, I should add. I declined the offer. The landlady shrugged. 'We had *Soldiers in Skirts* (an all-male revue) here last week,' she said, 'and they didn't mind sharing at all.'

Other digs were homely and comfortable, and I still correspond with landladies who were kind and helpful and who remember me from my days of near poverty. At times poverty was very close indeed as dates were scattered and money poor, twenty pounds less ten per cent commission being the average, and often dates only came in at the last moment when hope of a week's work had gone and the prospect of another week on the dole loomed.

On one occasion I was called at 10.30 on a Monday morning and asked by the doyen of variety agents, Billy Marsh (a man who guided many performers to stardom and who was the kingpin of London Management, the agency which booked most of the big American stars in the UK), if I was free to play for a week at the Palace Theatre, Preston – *that* week. The comic billed had had to drop out. It meant getting the next train from Euston, missing band call and arriving just in time for the first house. My fee was to be twenty-two pounds ten shillings for the week.

I accepted at once and started feverishly to pack. I duly played the date – and ever since, whenever we meet, Billy Marsh reminds me of the occasion. 'One of the highlights of your career,' he says. That week in Preston was interesting in one respect. The top of the bill was a man, famous throughout the variety profession, who billed himself as 'Kardomah – He fills the stage with flags', and indeed that's what he did. Starting from scratch he'd produce strings of flags, magician-style, from every part of his clothing. Then, moving to bigger things, he would entirely fill the stage from floor to flies with the flags of all nations while the pit orchestra played patriotic airs. It sounds corny and it was, but it was also strangely effective.

Between houses (it was twice-nightly variety) Kardomah could be seen through the open door of his dressing-room feverishly rolling up his flags and secreting them about his person in preparation for his next performance. He must have worked harder than the average manual worker, but he was after all in showbusiness!

One of the few young speciality acts I worked with were The Nelson Brothers, acrobatic dancers and violinists (a very amusing deadpan comedy act) with whom I struck up a friendship, but they soon departed for the continent where work was more plentiful and better paid. More often than not I found myself on the bill with elderly 'turns' who were totally out of touch with the modern world.

One elderly ventriloquist of the 'gottle of geer' school had bought the act of an even older vent, and saw nothing odd in mouthing jokes that had been current over thirty years before and singing a song that was popular in 1915.

Some of these old-timers were kind and helpful, but others were resentful of the newcomers whom they saw as a threat to their livelihood. In its last years variety (which was anything but) was a pathetic and inadequate form of entertainment that had outlived its purpose and had lost its audience to the more modern electronic media of radio and television. Alas, the old dogs of the music halls couldn't learn the new tricks of live radio and tv.

*

Now that it's dead and gone it's not easy to visualise a week on a variety bill in a strange town. Typically I would arrive in some gloomy hole on Sunday night, and walk from the railway station to my digs, lugging my suitcase. If lucky I'd be given supper and then go to bed. There seemed to be no form of entertainment available in the provinces on Sunday nights in the fifties, except watching others drinking in the dim and dreary pubs that were surprisingly numerous and generally about as welcoming as a mortuary.

On Monday morning I'd go to the theatre for band call where I'd meet the other acts on the bill and put my band parts down ready for rehearsal. It was first-come-first-served and the top of the bill had no priority over the juggling act or the bottom of the bill comic.

When my turn came I'd rehearse my music – opening signature tune and closing song – and then chat to the other acts. Sometimes they were complete strangers: foreign jugglers and trapeze artists or just people I'd never been on a bill with before. Others I knew from previous engagements. I'd then give my lighting plot, and directions about any special effects I wanted, to the chief electrician, discuss what kind of backing by way of scenery I needed (comedians usually got a backcloth of a street scene but I preferred drapes as they were less distracting to the audience) and tell the stage manager my on-and-off cues. He would then tell me how long my act was to last in order to ensure that the whole performance ran exactly to time. I think Ken Dodd was the only comedian never to pay heed to these instructions, which were common to all. He would keep going as long as the audience were laughing at him, and that could be a very long time indeed.

During these Monday morning happenings the theatre would be being cleaned and the debris of the previous Saturday's second house removed. One thing I do remember vividly is the smell of those Monday mornings. Orange peel and lysol mixed with the dust and the lingering memories of a hundred bygone animal acts (performing bears, seals, dogs and cats). Sometimes the morning was enlivened by the arrival of the local rodent exterminators who would move through the dressing-rooms pumping strange substances into any hole or crevice they could find.

Lunch, usually a pie and a pint at a nearby pub, would be followed, if in a new town, with a voyage of exploration. If you'd been there before the choice was the cinema or snooker hall. Snooker was cheap and the cinema often free to visiting thespians. You'd show your visiting card, known in the profession as the 'wilkie' (rhyming slang for card was a Wilkie Bard, named after the old comedian of that name). There was an expression used mainly by old repertory actors when seeking free admission to the cinema, 'Do you recognise the profession?' – a sonorous phrase I cherished although it's been nearly forty years since I've had the chance to use it.

First house Monday was invariably sticky unless the top of the bill was a crowd-puller. The audience consisted mainly of theatrical landladies and shop owners who received free tickets in exchange for exhibiting the bills advertising that week's attraction. They had seen it all and, not having had to pay, had little interest in the quality of the show.

But their word of mouth could make a lot of difference to the week's business. If they liked it they'd tell their customers – and if they didn't you'd be damned from one end of the town to the other, but playing to a houseful of local tradesmen was an ordeal that had to be faced, as had the rest of the week.

Twice-nightly variety could be fun, and if the audiences *did* like you the week passed in a pleasant glow. If, however, as happened to me in Wolverhampton where I didn't get a single laugh in twelve performances, it was very bleak. There was no knowing whether you'd go well or not, for in other theatres quite near Wolverhampton, for instance Tipton and Bearwood, my act went quite well. I was generally well-received in the south and south-west of England and in Wales, and once 'stopped the show' in Bedford, the audience enjoying my act so much they wouldn't cease applauding until I'd given an encore. Lancashire didn't care for me on the whole, and Yorkshire was totally unpredictable.

As time went on my act improved, but the only time I shared top of the bill was at Chester, with Shirley Bassey, then at the very beginning of her long and successful career. The audience, consisting largely of young servicemen stationed in the area, were vocal and enthusiastic. Shirley Bassey was gauche, and her voice was not fully mature; but you just knew, watching her, that she was a star. She was also good fun. It was a happy week.

Less happy was a week I played at the Shakespeare Theatre, Liverpool, one of three acts put in to strengthen the fading attractions of the striptease artiste Phyllis Dixey. She was supported by a troupe of girls and her husband, who specialised in low comedy and who rejoiced in the name of Snuffy Jack Tracey. This was 1955 and the aura of naughtiness that had made Miss Dixey a star had waned. In short, she wasn't a draw – hence the addition of three extra acts to beef up the show.

I was standing in the wings first house on Monday, ready to make my entrance as soon as the girls had finished the opening routine, when Phyllis Dixey fluttered up in a lacy dressing-gown and satin slippers and said to me in a terribly refined voice, 'I'm sorry but we don't allow people to stand in the wings during the performance. Would you kindly leave.' I said, 'I will if you wish, madam, but I'm the next act on.' She apologised and fluttered off. The week passed without further incident.

*

During my entire time 'working the halls', from 1953 to 1956, my fee was rarely higher than twenty pounds a week, although on one occasion I received thirty pounds and on another a staggering thirty-five. I played everywhere from the Candy Gardens in Guernsey to the Glasgow Empire, and life would have been grimmer but for the fact that by 1954 I started getting booked on a round of Sunday concerts supporting such stars as the American singer Billy Eckstein and they doubled my income at twenty pounds a Sunday. More than doubled it on one occasion when the promoter, Ed W. Jones, was so pleased with my performance he thrust an extra five pounds into my hand at the end of the evening.

I was now appearing fairly regularly on radio in such small-time programmes as *Up and Coming*, designed to encourage new talent, *Mid-day Music Hall*, in which acts of all kinds, young and old, appeared and where I encountered for the first time a delightful Australian producer, Trafford Whitelock, who was far from being the beer-swigging, corks-round-the-hat Aussie type. Quite the opposite in fact, and given to silk shirts in pastel shades, and winsome smiles.

On one occasion, censoring one of my jokes, he said 'Don't you think it's got a little too much S-E-X?' He was too fastidious to come out with the actual word, and I saw the possibilities in a character based on him and introduced it into *Pertwee's Progress* with some success.

On my travels around the music halls I met Marty Feldman and we formed a friendship that lasted until he died nearly twenty years later, but my relationship with Marty and our work together deserves and has a chapter of its own.

Strangely enough, although he was an extremely courteous, shrewd and decent man, my agent Sonny Zahl never felt that I was particularly talented, and had difficulty in selling me. But thanks to Stanley Dale and various night-club owners (including Clement Freud who, in those days, owned a club over the Royal Court Theatre in Sloane Square) I worked regularly doing cabaret spots at the Royal Court, Esmerelda's Barn in Knightsbridge – which it turned out much later was owned and patronised by the Kray twins. The Grill Room at the Dorchester Hotel also featured cabaret, and I did a month there; I played the Blue Angel in Berkeley Street where later David Frost was discovered, the Ace of Clubs in the basement of Izow's restaurant in Brewer Street, the Cascade in Stratton Street where nobody came, and Quaglino's on more than one occasion.

At Quaglino's I acquired an unexpected fan. Earl Mountbatten of Burma, who came one evening with his wife, liked my act and invited me over for a drink when I'd finished. He was fascinated by the name Took and when I couldn't explain its origins he insisted that it and I were Dutch. He came more than once afterwards, always invited me for a drink and chatted amiably to me on every occasion.

I wasn't so popular with the 'in' crowd at Clement Freud's club, who were Chris Chataway, Chris Brasher, Roger Bannister and others of that Oxbridge set of doctors, politicians and athletes. At first they liked what I did, but Freud used me so often (for £15 a week, or £1.50 a night if I stood in for somebody else) that when they were gathered in the downstairs bar and I appeared on my way up to perform they would groan and go elsewhere. I made great friends with the waiters and the chef, however, and always got a good meal. Not only that but the waiters refused to serve anyone while I was on, so that I had the undivided attention of the audience.

Appearing at the Sloane Square club did have its down side.

Freud had the strange habit of using bits of my act in his introduction. Once, when he had used a full five-minute sequence from the heart of my routine, my opening line was 'Welcome to the Royal Court, Sloane Square, the only club in London where the proprietor is funnier than the cabaret.' Years later he confided to me that one of my jokes from those days was still 'going awfully well'! Freud, a passionate anti-smoker, naturally found it apt. The joke was this: 'There's a new brand of cigarettes on the market. They're called McWhirters. They're so foul that they've formed a group called M.A. McWhirters Anonymous. If you get the desire to smoke one you phone a special number, a member comes round to your home and you get drunk together.' Good luck, Sir Clement, long may you get laughs with it.

I tended in those days to get bored with my routines and write myself new ones – not always terribly successful, and club- or theatre-owners would plead with me to go back to my old routine. I even learned to sing and dance when at the Dorchester, which must have been a pretty revolting spectacle. No wonder that one night a heckler called from the back of the room, 'Why don't you wash your hands in molten lead?' A cheery remark from a member of the British upper classes, I'm sure you'll agree.

By the time I was making regular appearances in West End cabaret (1956–57) my fortunes had taken an upturn elsewhere. In 1956, thanks to another Fosters agent, Bob Heath (son of band leader, Ted Heath), who was standing in for Sonny Zahl, I auditioned for the intimate revue *For Amusement Only* which was being planned to follow the success of the same team's *Intimacy at Eight*, which had run for some time at the Criterion Theatre in Piccadilly Circus.

I was one of many at the audition. They were mainly girls, and in fact, without my knowing it, the male cast had already been set. The audition was taken by the show's musical director and principal composer, Ronnie Cass, and I cracked my jokes and sang something awful and raised a lot of laughs from the other auditionees.

Ronnie Cass and the representatives of the management – Linnit and Dunfee – must have liked what they saw because I was asked to return that afternoon and perform for the show's principal author, Peter Myers. I duly reappeared on the stage at the time agreed, announced laconically 'Act Two, Same as Act One' and went into my routine. I got the job, and the show ran at the Apollo Theatre in Shaftesbury Avenue for over seven hundred performances. When it finally closed I was asked to appear in its successor, *For Adults Only*. That ran for a year, and at its close my theatrical career came to an end.

Well, almost. In 1986 I appeared in a Charity Show at the Theatre Royal, Drury Lane, in a sketch written by Marty and me called 'Funny He Never Married' in which Tim Brooke-Taylor and I played two old men reminiscing about a third whose funeral they'd just attended. Not having been on stage for nearly thirty years my make-up was somewhat extreme, and I heard John Cleese, who was also appearing in the show, saying to Peter Cook 'Who is that strange man in the corner rubbing his hands and mumbling to himself?' (I was doing this for Cleese's benefit, I might add.) Cook said, 'Oh, that's Barry', at which Cleese came over, peered at me, saw it was me and hissed 'You are a bloody fool, Took.'

In the 1950s the West End proved a lot easier than provincial variety and the cast of *For Amusement Only* bulged with talent. Although in theory Ronnie Stevens was the leading man, Ron Moody took most of the honours having, to be fair, most of the better parts. Hugh Paddick was quite brilliant too, in addition to being one of the nicest men in the business (and still going strong today in his seventies). The other men in the Company were Jimmy Thompson and Michael Charnley, who was also the choreographer. My dancing was so inept he christened me Godzilla, but in the rough-and-tumble of revue my un-Nijinskyesque caperings went unnoticed. The ladies in the Company were strong too: Thelma Ruby, Dilys Laye, Vivienne Martin, Barbara Young, Audrey Nicholson and nineteen-year-old Judy Carne who danced like thistledown but was in every other way incredibly clumsy and, in the blackouts that followed the various sketches in which she appeared, would crash into the scenery or other actors in a reckless and life-endangering way, an early preparation for her *Rowan and Martin's Laugh In* role as the Sock It To Me girl.

I played small parts, mainly old men and policemen, and generally entered to utter the pay-off line of the sketch. So much so that the stage hands christened me 'tag-line Took'. I did have one major role, playing a variety of bandleaders through the ages in a number called 'Dance Sensations', the climax of which was a quartet consisting of Hugh Paddick on piano, Jimmy Thompson on drums, Ron Moody on banjo and me on trumpet belting out 'Balling the Jack' while Michael Charnley and Noel Rossana danced to a spinning, whirling climax.

As the months went on and new material was added I found I had more to do, and by that time Ronnie Cass and I had become firm friends and I spent a lot of time at his home in Ordnance Hill, St John's Wood. He wrote original music for my cabaret act and made arrangements of what was not his own original work. He also accompanied me at auditions and couldn't have been more helpful to a young man with a fair amount of talent but with a large economy-size inferiority complex. His wife, Valerie, was wonderful to me too. She was a beautiful young woman who had been stunning in an earlier revue, *High Spirits*, and who had met and married Ronnie when he was the musical director of the show.

The three of us were Scrabble addicts and after rehearsing with Ronnie for my next cabaret date he'd always suggest a game. Valerie was roped in and away we'd go, thoroughly absorbed in the word game. So much so that one Saturday afternoon we suddenly realised that it was less than half an hour to curtain up at the Apollo.

Ronnie and I raced for the theatre (a twenty-minute journey away). I dashed up to my dressing-room and changed rapidly for the opening number, while Ronnie played the longest Overture in the history of intimate revue.

Our friendship aside, one of his favourite pastimes was to make me laugh during the performance. He'd do this in a variety of ways from changing key in the middle of a musical number to creating the sound of a body being dragged along the floor of the orchestra pit while I was in full flood. When, as was called for in my contract, I understudied various members of the Company when they were off, he would play completely different tunes or double the speed of the regular numbers. I reached a point where I got the giggles so easily that I had to go to the doctor for tablets to quieten me down.

My retaliation to Ronnie and the small orchestra which accompanied the show, and who joined in heartily with his cheerful sadism was not to laugh, but the absurdity of my covering for Jimmy Thompson in a number created for him where he impersonated Liberace was too much for me, Ronnie or the audience, many of whom came regularly to the show, to take seriously. I was six feet two and thin, and even with padded evening dress and a wig looked nothing like the glitzy Polish/American entertainer. I would look soulfully at the audience and say 'If you'll believe this you'll believe anything' and then go into the routine. Or I'd go off into an impersonation of Victor Borge, who was appearing in his one-man show at the time at the Palace Theatre just up the road.

Most of these antics took place during matinees when there were few people in to complain. Ron Moody was particularly inventive and wore the most extraordinary costumes and make-up at these afternoon shows, and Hugh Paddick and Ronnie Stevens would, on occasion, ad lib in some hilarious way. Hugh's best gag was to attach a small moustache box, disguised to look like a deaf aid, to his chest and have a string leading from that to his ear. This simulated hearing appliance would come into play at will and he had a number of variations on its use.

The rest of the cast, or at any rate those who enjoyed the joke, would shout the lines at his chest and Hugh would nod benignly, pretending not to have heard a word until, with an adjustment of his device he would indicate that he was hearing loud and clear. I, of course, would get the giggles and a certain amount of mayhem would ensue with the Company Manager threatening dire punishments and the more sober members of the cast complaining bitterly that their performances were being ruined.

In a long run, however, it is essential to find any means of keeping the comedy fresh, and that we did.

*

During my time with *For Amusement Only* I was amazed to find that I had a fan. Her name was Biddy and she was a waitress in the sandwich bar in Rupert Street, off Shaftesbury Avenue, where, after rehearsals or before the show, you could pop in for any one of a choice of dozens of exotic sandwich fillings. Biddy had, unknown to me, not only been to see *For Amusement Only* several times but she'd also been to every nightclub in which I'd ever appeared and had collected every press cutting in which my name was mentioned. One day she shyly presented me with a book of cuttings and mementoes of my performances.

I'm not the sort of person who attracts hero worship and this single-minded cataloguing of my career amazed me. I was, and am, deeply grateful to Biddy and sad, looking back, that I could not reciprocate her devotion.

She chronicled, among other things, a tv disaster I was involved with called *Round About Ten*. There's not much to be said about it. Jack Jackson, bandleader turned disc jockey turned tv presenter had a very successful series, *The Jack Jackson Show*. Naturally he wanted a summer break and ATV, the producing company, were looking for something that could fill the late-night Sunday spot. At that time I was doing a number of Sunday concerts and on one I appeared on the same bill as Barbara Lyon, daughter of Bebe Daniels and Ben Lyon. They were great friends of Mr and Mrs Val Parnell, and Val Parnell ran ATV. Mrs Val Parnell had been to the concert to hear Barbara Lyon sing, so she couldn't avoid seeing my act too. The outcome was that I was recommended to Val Parnell, I made a pilot programme which he liked and I was duly booked to appear in the Jack Jackson replacement which was called *Round About Ten*. Alas, the series didn't live up to the promise of the pilot, and although it also featured such excellent performers as Jim Dale and Jimmy Young (in those days at the height of his singing career) *Round About Ten* was one of those shows that everyone connected with it would prefer to forget, and in no time at all it was forgotten.

At some point in the run of *For Amusement Only* Jimmy Thompson was replaced by Wallas Eaton, a stalwart of the radio series *Take It From Here*, Noel Rossana by Katie Feather and Dilys Laye by Pat Lancaster, who later became a regular in *Beyond Our Ken*. At a reunion in 1986, organised by Thelma Ruby, to celebrate the 30th anniversary of the first rehearsal of

For Amusement Only almost all the cast turned up (only Hugh Paddick and Dilys Laye were absent) and the talent and energy in that group thirty years on was remarkable.

Helen Cotterill, a sweet and chubby lass, then an understudy, has since made her living as an actress. Thelma Ruby is married to a magnificent cook and author, Peter Frye. Ron Moody became an international star with his portrayal of Fagin in Lionel Bart's *Oliver*. Barbara Young appears regularly in West End stage shows and on tv. Hugh Paddick became an outstanding member of the cast of *Beyond Our Ken* and *Round the Horne* and many other shows besides on stage and tv. Dilys Laye is rarely off radio. Pat Lancaster spends much of her time at sea singing on cruise liners.

They are a talented bunch who helped to keep the West End alive when theatre was thought to be in decline. In fact, *For Amusement Only* became extremely popular with many of the Hollywood stars visiting London who, on the urging of Jack Benny, a frequent visitor and a great fan of the show, came to the Apollo and in turn became fans too.

I remember meeting Van Johnson, Sam Goldwyn, Tyrone Power and Charles Laughton, not to mention Marcel Marceau who invited me to join his company in Paris, and the cast of the French revue, *La Plume de ma Tante*, which played a season in London during our run and for whom we gave a party.

On our own last night I can remember clearly Charles Laughton in tears saying, 'But why must it end – it's so lovely.'

Lovely to the onlooker possibly; but after several hundred performances, for the cast the loveliness tends to wear off.

The authors and composers – Ronnie Cass, Peter Myers, Stanley Myers, John Pritchett (Pat Lancaster's husband), Richard Waring, Alan Melville and Donald Swann – were brisk and alert, and combined their talents in a remarkable way. Nothing was to be seen like *For Amusement Only* until *Beyond the Fringe* appeared several years later on the West End scene. Before that we had to endure *For Adults Only*, which – not to be too rude about it – was a cock-up from the beginning.

For a start Linnit and Dunfee were no longer the management. It was a consortium formed around Robert Morley and theatrical agent Robin Fox (father of Edward, James and

Robert) in association with S.A. Gorlinsky. The concept was magnificent, but, to adapt the French reaction to the Charge of the Light Brigade, 'C'était magnifique mais ce n'était pas la Revue Intime.'

The intention was that two matinee matrons of the type that clatter tea trays and gossip throughout afternoon performances would obliquely compère the show, commenting on the action. Then there was a second theme of two bright-eyed youngsters, played by Richard Waring and Louie Ramsay. Into this formula the sketches were pushed like threepenny bits into a Christmas pudding. The whole thing was top heavy and unworkable, and to add to the disaster the set was made of dark brown imitation suede, which did not reflect light. Whatever wattage was used and however many lamps were employed, that frightful set seemed to swallow it all and remain as dull as before.

We started our pre-London tour at the New Theatre Oxford, and after a nightmarish eight-hour dress rehearsal on Sunday opened on the Monday to a wave of indifference from the audience that is hard to describe. The show looked awful and sounded awful, and after that first night everything but the musical numbers was cut.

The rest of the week went by in a nightmare of rewrites, new running orders and new sketches which fared as badly as the old, to the general despair of the cast. Slowly and painfully in the weeks that followed order emerged out of chaos, and by the time we reached Glasgow a month later the show wasn't at all bad.

We opened in London at the Strand Theatre on 25 June 1958, and by then many of the cast had gone – much of the continuity had disappeared, we had a new set and new sketches had been written. I contributed one based on a BBC tv series of the day, *You are There* – which recreated famous moments of history (e.g. The Last Days of Pompeii). My version was 'You are there at the Last Days of Sodom and Gomorrah'. Asked by the BBC interviewer 'Are you one of the City Fathers', I forgot the line I had written and ad libbed in an upper-class drawl, 'I shouldn't be at all surprised.' Amazingly it brought the house down, and the show soon got into its stride with first-rate performances from Miriam Karlin, Ron Moody and Hugh Paddick as Alec

Guinness in a series of sketches about Oscar-winning films. In one of these sketches Richard Waring and I disgraced ourselves totally and caused poor Louie Ramsay to dissolve into tears.

The premise was that Louie was Shirley Temple, Richard Waring was her plantation-owning father and I was their black servant, Old Boll Weevil. The sketch opened with an exchange of pleasantries between master and man about life in the deep south and the talents of young Missie. Then Missie would trip on, master and servant would exit and the Shirley Temple figure would sing and dance a tongue-in-cheek version of a typically nauseating Shirley Temple song.

That was the theory. In practice the sketch was chronically weak and, in addition, by now some weeks into the run, Richard Waring, himself a great giggler, decided that it presented a good opportunity to make me 'corpse', the theatrical phrase for laughing aloud and out of context.

So, as the lovable old Negro retainer rocked the Colonel gently in the rocking chair, Waring said, 'Tell me, Cohen ...' Now, if I had laughed, all would have been well; but by the use of iron self-control I kept silent. Waring was so taken aback that he burst into shrieks of laughter himself and when they died down I walked to the footlights and said in my best Whitechapel accent, 'Cohen? Haven't I got enough trouble being black?' More shrieks from Waring, who just managed to choke out the cue for Louie Ramsay to enter before disappearing hurriedly into the wings, with me close behind.

In the weeks that followed we developed the routine, until quite often we would improvise a cross-talk act for several minutes before the unfortunate Miss Ramsay could come on. Needless to say, Richard Waring and I were severely reprimanded for this unprofessional behaviour, but the audience enjoyed our banter and there were few enough jokes in the original script.

Eventually that sketch was dropped, for when played straight it went for nothing, but Richard Waring and I continued our war of nerves, each trying to make the other laugh. That all sounds very amateurish, but it was an awful show and the ad libbing helped to relieve the tension. *For Adults Only* ran for about a year and was not a total flop at the box office, but I believe that its demise signalled the end of the old camp West End revue. The audience's expectations had changed and we had become, it must be admitted, old hat.

*

By the time *For Adults Only* had run its course I had left Fosters Agency and joined Associated London Scripts whose directors, as well as Stanley Dale, included Tony Hancock, Frankie Howerd, Spike Milligan, Eric Sykes, and Alan Simpson and Ray Galton. Having been writing with Eric Merriman for some time – ghosting it was called, as my name didn't appear on any credits – I thought it was a sensible move to join the leading scriptwriting agency, and when in 1957 Merriman (who was already a client) and I were commissioned to write a pilot show for Kenneth Horne, my name went on the script. At the same time Eric was working with a Scottish writer, Lew Schwartz, and as they were busy I was set the task of devising a title for the new Horne show. Eric had wanted to call it Hornerama, which in fact one segment came to be called, in theory at least a parody of tv's current affairs show, *Panorama*. I preferred *Round the Horne* (which it subsequently became when Marty Feldman and I took over), but I put up a list of about six alternatives, including *Beyond Our Ken*, which was the one the BBC preferred, and that's what the show was called.

From *For Adults Only* we recruited Hugh Paddick, Ron Moody and Patricia Lancaster. Eric had been writing for Betty Marsden on tv and she joined the cast too. Then by lucky chance Kenneth Williams became available. He'd spent years with *Hancock's Half Hour*, but a change of format had made him redundant (or rather Hancock wouldn't work with him any more) and we were asked if we would like him in the cast too. Of course we were delighted and wrote our pilot script.

The BBC were pleased with it, but before we could embark on a series Kenneth Horne suffered a stroke and the project was delayed until 1958. In the interim Merriman and I wrote some tv specials, and as I was still in the theatre and playing cabarets most nights, I didn't see much home life.

Dot and I with our young family were able to move from our flat in Church Crescent to a four-bedroom semi in Creighton Avenue, Muswell Hill for which I paid £4350, helped by Stanley Dale who lent me £1500. My Hillman Minx was replaced by a Jaguar and, most important, we'd had another child, a girl this time, named Susan.

When *Beyond Our Ken* did start it was an immediate success and soon had its catchphrases, 'The answer lies in the soil', 'Thirty-five years', and 'Hello Rodney, Hello Charles.' Eric Merriman and I wrote most of the script, but Kenneth Horne contributed a fair amount too, including an accident-prone BBC reporter, Cecil Snaith. Kenneth Horne was a great deviser of funny names and would often sign letters Chas Tittibelt, or Gladys Harbinger. He was a sweet, wry, funny man.

He and Richard Murdoch had been responsible for the long-running *Much Binding in the Marsh*, and together had assembled a massive list of credits. In addition, Kenneth was involved in a number of panel games and he was the ideal chairman, genial and urbane.

After his stroke in 1957 he resigned from most of his business commitments (he'd been Sales Director of Triplex Glass, MD of British Industries Fair and a director of various other companies) but stuck to his show-business work and travelled all over the country appearing on radio and tv shows. *Beyond Our Ken* became one of his most important programmes and the supporting cast gave this lovable man their all.

After the first series Ron Moody was replaced by Bill Pertwee, but otherwise the show remained much the same: three sketches broken up by two singing spots, the first by Pat Lancaster, the second by the Fraser Hayes Four. The BBC Variety Orchestra and the BBC Revue Orchestra played for alternate series.

Then, as later, I found that I was a reasonably good collaborator on a script but tended to be impatient when the tempo of writing slowed.

Merriman had a large collection of gag books to which he constantly referred. Mainly they were collections made by the American writer, or should I say assembler of jokes, Robert Orben, and Merriman would search through these slim volumes looking for a joke that would fit the sketch or scene we were writing. Towards the end of our writing relationship I began to resent this use of second-hand material, feeling that it would have been quicker and infinitely better to invent new stuff.

*

Beyond Our Ken became so popular that when Frank Muir and Denis Norden were poached by BBC Television to become Comedy Advisers, and BBC Radio was left with the awkward situation of a top series, *Take It From Here*, but no one to write it, they turned to Merriman and me.

At the time (1959) it was considered an accolade, but personally I doubted if we could do it. After all, Muir and Norden were at that time among the best, and certainly the most experienced script writers going and *TIFH*, as it was known, had been one of post-war radio's big successes.

During the last series written by Muir and Norden, Merriman and I had a number of meetings with them. Denis Norden was particularly helpful, guiding us through the pitfalls of writing for the team of Dick Bentley, Jimmy Edwards and June Whitfield. As we wrote sample sketches which Denis Norden 'corrected' it dawned on me that Merriman and I were pulling in different directions and that the results were likely to be disappointing, if not downright disastrous. I confided this to Norden and expressed my frustration. To my intense surprise he became quite vehement about *his* frustrations writing with Frank Muir.

Later I became aware that *all* writing partnerships suffer from frustration and mutual irritation, for however much you like the person you're writing with – and it's like marriage without the sex – the daily grind of invention leads to impatience, irritation and eventually a parting of the ways. The friendship doesn't diminish, but the ability to write together goes. There are exceptions, of course. Ronnie Wolfe and Ronnie Chesney (who wrote *The Rag Trade* for Reg Varney, Peter Jones, Miriam Karlin, Sheila Hancock and others), and *On the Buses* (again for Reg Varney and a talented cast) are one such combination, but offhand I can think of no others.

Frank Muir always used to claim that any writing partnership could only last ten years. By comparison my partnership with Eric Merriman lasted ten minutes. As we neared the deadline of *TIFH* so our mutual dislike and frustration increased and writing sessions tended to lapse into sullen silence.

The bosses of Radio Light Entertainment at that time were Pat Hillyard as head of the department and Jim Davidson as his number two. Hillyard was an urbane, somewhat aloof man who had been crucial in the post-war development of BBC Radio comedy; Jim Davidson was an Australian with a matter-of-fact, down-market view of entertainment and people. His suggestion to solve the Merriman/Took impasse was that we should take our coats off, go into the back alley behind Aeolian Hall and slug it out in a fist fight.

Naturally enough no one else saw this as a realistic solution to the problem, and the matter was solved in an arrangement whereby Eric Merriman would write the middle sketch and I, with Marty Feldman, would do the first and the last, featuring the Glums (a continuing story of the courtship of a gormless lad, Ron (Dick Bentley) and a naive girl, Eth (June Whitfield) hampered by Ron's greedy, selfish father, Pa Glum (Jimmy Edwards).

If a writer has any talent at all he rejoices when the cast enhance his work, and the team of Bentley, Edwards and June Whitfield were first-class. At that time the actor Bernard Miles was building the Mermaid Theatre at Puddle Dock by Blackfriars Bridge, a noble, exciting and, in commercial terms, dangerous project. Marty and I echoed that by having Dick Bentley launch a comparable, and of course totally fictitious, project. Scripting the Glums came easily, as it had been so carefully and beautifully written in the past by Frank and Denis. We reintroduced Mrs Glum (previously she'd been played intentionally incoherently by Alma Cogan) as a sound effect of slippered feet slouching across a kitchen floor, and a door slamming. Pa Glum would say things like 'Mother, how many times have I told you to take your cap off when you're indoors?' The idea worked at first but tended to hold up the action and we dropped it after a few episodes.

The story built up to the Glum family emigrating to Australia and finding themselves, in the last episode, on the Woolwich Ferry.

There had been other changes in *TIFH* too. With the departure of Frank Muir and Denis Norden, the long-standing producer Charles Maxwell had also left to take on other radio shows and his place was taken by Charles Chilton who, in his own right, was probably the most brilliant writer and producer in the history of world radio (with the possible exception of Orson Welles) and whose western serial *Riders of the Range* and science fiction epic *Journey into Space* became classics, was never more than professionally interested in *Take It From Here*.

When the series ended – with a sigh of relief all round – Marty and I were well-established and Eric Merriman and I never wrote together again. Not that we would ever have wished to, for although it was for a time a mutually profitable experience our different personalities and attitudes would have made a long relationship impossible.

When the next series of *Beyond Our Ken* was scheduled I received a letter from Kenneth Horne saying that, much as he regretted it, I was being dropped for the greater good of the show. That is to say Eric Merriman had refused to work with me and had said, 'It's either Took or me.' As he was the acknowledged senior writer, it was felt that in everyone's interests the choice should be Merriman and not Took. I felt hurt at the time by this rebuff as I had contributed a lot to *Beyond Our Ken*, but the hurt was tempered by the fact that Marty and I had as much work as we could handle.

*

Among the flops and the successes of a long career I've had a couple of 'nearlys'. One nearly was when I *nearly* replaced Kenneth Williams as general purpose character man in the radio version of *Hancock's Half Hour*. Kenneth was busy filming and was unavailable for some recordings. Dennis Main Wilson, the producer, was keen for me to take over and arranged for me to meet Tony Hancock in a pub off Bond Street. We duly met, got on well and after imbibing a few beers parted amicably.

I didn't get the job and, in fact, not long afterwards Kenneth Williams left *Hancock's Half Hour* for good and was never replaced.

Another nearly was when I was going strong in the weekly tv show *Late Extra*. Max Bygraves was starring in a revue at the London Palladium and planned to take a holiday. I was invited to understudy him and play in his sketches if (or undoubtedly *when*) he was 'off'. I pointed out to the agent concerned, another of the Foster's Agency team, Max Kester (the former writer and BBC producer), that the money offered, £30 per week, was less than I was getting for my tv appearances (£40 per programme). Clearly I would have to give up the tv spot if I was to take the Bygraves understudy role. But I said I would do it if I could also do my solo act in the show. It would have been a wonderful showcase and could have led to greater things, whereas appearing in a couple of indifferent sketches would do me no good at all professionally. Answer came that this was unacceptable to the management, and when Max Bygraves did take a holiday he was replaced by Gracie Fields's brother, Tommy, a light comedian. And so through 1959 I continued happily with *Late Extra*. 'Happily' because apart from the fact that I had weekly exposure on tv I came into contact with several heroes of mine whom I'd never have met otherwise.

Late Extra was the first-ever late-night chat show on tv, mounted by Associated Rediffusion, and I, playing the part of a barman in the night club setting, was there to provide topical jokes either briefly, if the chat with the main guests overran, or at great length if someone didn't turn up. The show was live and had to fit exactly to the time scheduled for the commercial breaks.

It worked well on the whole; the first host was Edmund Purdom, the film star, but he was subsequently replaced by two experienced tv interviewers, Nick Barker and Kenneth McLeod.

The guests I remember most vividly were Richard Rogers and Oscar Hammerstein II, Margery Allingham, the mystery writer, Nicholas Monsarrat, author of the best-selling *The Cruel Sea*, and William Saroyan, the Armenian/American writer whose work I'd always loved, author of *The Man on the Flying Trapeze*. After each programme there was sumptuous hospitality, and the chance to chat to those heroic figures was enchanting.

When I left the show after a year to go to work for Granada

Television, my place was taken by the elegant Basil Boothroyd and the show was hosted by the best-known tv cook of the time, Fanny Craddock. The night club setting was replaced by a more elegant drawing-room and I can remember Fanny Craddock, who was no great shakes as an interviewer, having a particularly difficult time with Sir Gerald Kelly (at that time President of the Royal Academy) and saying at last, in desperation, 'For God's sake, Gerald, say something, if it's only goodnight.'

7

Marty and Me

I had the mitigated pleasure of working with Marty Feldman for ten years – and I'll explain my reservations presently – but the unmitigated pleasure of knowing him as a friend for very much longer. We first met in 1954 and were friends until his untimely death in 1982.

I never really discovered much about his early childhood. He talked vaguely about his father being called up and the family moving from the East End of London to Luton. He remembered with horror a boarding school he'd been sent to where the food was awful and you were beaten if you didn't eat it, of running away from home at the age of fifteen to join a Wild West Show in Margate, and of coming to hate the restrictions of a middle-class Jewish family life in north London. Marty's father was a small, neat, twinkling-eyed gown manufacturer, affectionately known as Mossy. Marty's mother was very much the Jewish matriarch: a big, commanding woman, deep-voiced and decisive. Marty, when I first met him, was a sweet-faced lad of twenty-one with a not unsightly broken nose obtained during his schooldays seeing off a bully, and a small goatee beard, which he'd grown as a tribute to his great hero, Dizzy Gillespie the jazz trumpet player.

We first met at the York Empire in '54. Marty had put together an act with another Jewish youngster, Morris Sellar, and a third lad, Mitch Gribble, which was a crazy knockabout turn based partly on Marx Brothers comedy and partly on Olsen and Johnson's *Hellzapoppin*.

The act finished with them playing the number 'Crazy Rhythm' with Mitch on drums, Morris on guitar and Marty on trumpet. The act was called Morris, Marty and Mitch, and it was dreadful. Admittedly Mitch was a good drummer and some of their gags got laughs, but on the whole they were about as much like the Marx Brothers as the Mormon Tabernacle Choir.

At the York Empire I had been booked for the week as bottom-of-the-bill stand-up comic and they shared bottom billing. On the Monday morning band call they discovered that they were second turn on, straight after the two-girl tap-dancing act, while I was due to appear after the interval.

They complained at first to the manager and then their agent, but the placings stood and they, with the worst spot on the bill, were incensed. Naturally after the interval the audience had warmed up a little and responded better and so my act was quite well received, while Morris, Marty and Mitch suffered horribly. Not only were they not very good but as they were young and far from experienced, the York audiences were baffled by their clumsily delivered, largely incomprehensible jokes.

The act, I should point out, consisted mainly of cross-overs. Marty would walk across the stage with a suitcase. Mitch would ask 'Where are you going?' Marty would reply, 'I'm taking this case to court.' He'd exit. Morris would cross from the other side, with an axe buried in a false cranium, complaining 'I've got a splitting headache.' Marty would return with the suitcase and a ladder. Mitch would ask, 'Where are you going now?' Marty would say, 'I'm taking this case to a higher court'... and so on.

On the face of it not much worse than many other bottom-of-the-bill acts, but it was clear that only Marty had any flair for comedy. The week that had started with us as deadly enemies ended with our being great friends. Marty and I discovered that we had much in common.

We were both mediocre trumpet players who had aspired to play in dance bands but who hadn't made the grade. Both of us had dropped out of school at fifteen. Both of us came from ultra-respectable families, for although my family was not Jewish the conformity was of much the same order as in Marty's family. Furthermore, our homes were only a few miles from each other. I was five years older than Marty and though our personalities were different our attitudes and beliefs were almost identical.

The next week both acts were booked at the Knightstone Theatre, Weston-super-Mare, and by then Marty and I were inseparable. We'd meet every morning at the theatre, go for walks together and talk endlessly.

On Wednesday we had a conversation that was to change my performing career if not for good then at least for the better. Marty said, 'You look much funnier off the stage than on it.' I thought he was kidding, but no. He said, 'Look, on the stage you wear a lounge suit like every other stand-up comic and you tell the same sort of jokes. In the street you wear a sports jacket and slacks, a cheese-cutter cap, your old school tie and an umbrella. Why don't you go on wearing that lot? Try it and see.'

The prospect alarmed and excited me. That night I dreamed an opening line, 'I expect you're wondering why I sent for you', and the next evening first house, dressed as I had been for the street, I went on, leaned nonchalantly on my umbrella and said the line. The sheer impertinence of it made the audience titter. I then said, 'I'd like to make it quite clear before I go any further that I am not an American.' Coming from this stereotyped Englishman the audience found that funny too and, in short, my act went better than it had ever gone before.

As the week went on Marty, acting as Svengali to my cloth-capped Trilby, helped me polish my routine so that by the end of the engagement I was doing very well.

Some weeks of unemployment followed and, while I had a little money, Marty had none at all. He did however have a car which his father had given him for his twenty-first birthday, and when I had the price of a gallon or two of petrol (I think in those days it was £1 – for four gallons) we'd drive around, and when I got the odd engagement in club or pub Marty would act as my chauffeur.

While Marty's help meant that my act was now more bookable, and indeed quite successful, he was unable to do much to improve Morris, Marty and Mitch and after a few dates and a tv appearance in the Jimmy Wheeler show, which was produced by Brian Tesler, the act quietly folded. Meanwhile I had graduated to the Moss tour, which meant the big Empire Theatres that dotted the country.

By the time I reached the Empire, Edinburgh, in 1955, my act was set and as good as it was ever going to be, and the top of the bill at Edinburgh, Ella Logan (Aunt of Jimmy Logan) fresh from Hollywood and making a triumphant return to her native Scotland, thought it was brilliant. So much so that she insisted that I be included in the following week's show at the Glasgow Empire. I was unbilled and clearly puzzled the Glaswegian rowdies, who traditionally hated any English comedian, and so I got away with it; but the manager disliked me on sight and paid me my thirty pounds salary on the Friday night banging one £1 note after another onto the dressing-room table as if each was a fist he was thumping into my face.

*

It was in those two weeks in Scotland that I met two more men whose lives were to join Marty's and mine in an important way. Their names were Bill Craig and John Law, and they both worked for the *Scottish Daily Express*. More than that, however, they wrote radio comedy scripts for a northern Ireland comedian, James Young (no relation of singer, DJ and chat-show host Jimmy Young) and material for Glasgow pantomimes. They also offered to write material for any passing comedian, and *that's* how we met. I don't think I ever bought any material from them, but Bill, John and I became close friends and when shortly after the Glasgow dates I hit another bad patch of unemployment, they offered to get me a job on the *Scottish Daily Express*.

Fortunately things bucked up for me soon after, and for Bill and John too, as in 1956 they got a contract to write 'scripts of all descriptions' for ATV, one of the new ITV companies. The most important show they wrote was *Joan and Leslie*, starring Joan and Leslie Randall, alternating with the writing team Dick Sharples and Gerald Kelsey and creating one of the first sit-coms on ITV. In the event Bill Craig did most of the sit-com writing in their partnership and John, who didn't really care for sit-com, did the variety work: jokes and wheezes, sketches and quickies for such emerging jokesmiths as Morecambe and Wise.

Bill was married and he and his wife, Alro (short for Alice Rose), set up house in a vast apartment in a house in Willesden, while John had a bachelor apartment in Linden Gardens, Notting Hill.

When, in 1956, I was established in a dressing-room at the Apollo Theatre, John and Marty became constant visitors. They also became firm friends, and Marty, who was also single, and John spent a lot of time together. Their great speciality was to make private recordings on John's tape recorder – totally scurrilous versions of popular radio and tv shows of the day. After the curtain came down on the night's performance at the Apollo I'd travel to John Law's apartment in Notting Hill and listen to these two young iconoclasts' latest piece of crazy nonsense.

In 1956 ITV was in its infancy and its studios were mostly converted theatres. My old stamping ground, Wood Green Empire, was now a tv studio, as was Hackney Empire where ATV produced a number of afternoon programmes.

Marty Feldman and I wrote and appeared in these shows in a variety of spoofs and Bill Craig contributed one piece of nonsense involving a picture sequence of me and Baron von Richtofen. Our humour was often obscure and adventurous and, it must be said, not terribly funny; but our producer, Anna Lett (then married to Chris Chataway), was charming and easy-going and was only too happy to help these cheery young men to learn the complex business of television.

By 1959 Marty was part of the team, along with Ronnie Wolfe and Ronnie Chesney, writing *Educating Archie* (and hating it) and I was toiling away at *Beyond Our Ken*. Both of us were unhappy with what we were doing but enjoyed each other's company and shared a sense of humour.

The fracas over *Take It From Here* meant that we started actively to write together professionally and that led to our being offered other work. From Granada the occasional episode of *The Army Game*, from Charles Maxwell a commission to write the second series of a radio show called *We're In Business*. This starred Harry Worth and Peter Jones, Irene Handl and Dick Emery with small parts played by Ian McNaughton, who was later to become a tv director with shows like *Monty Python's Flying Circus* and *Rising Damp* to his credit.

In a typical week Marty and I would write two segments of

Take It From Here, two thirds of *We're In Business* and an episode of *The Army Game*, and in addition there'd be *Educating Archie* (Marty only) and *Late Extra* (me only).

We wrote fast, but all this work was physically beyond us and we recruited Bill Craig who also had a heavy work schedule – mainly episodes of straight series like *Deadline Midnight* and *Dixon of Dock Green*, and later his own glorious recreation of the days of the puffer boats on the Clyde, *The Vital Spark* – to help out with *We're In Business*.

We'd meet in Bill's home, discuss the episode we had to write, divide the story into three segments, go into separate rooms and write. When that was done – some hours later – we'd reconvene in Bill's study and I would dictate to Bill, editing as I went, and he would type the final version, with Marty adding extra gags as we went along. It sounds odd, but because the three of us, although totally different from each other, found a great rapport, the scripts were remarkably good. They were also improved greatly by Peter Jones, who wrote the preamble to each week's episode. Here's an example:

DUDLEY: (PETER JONES)	Another week has passed since I last had the pleasure of addressing you. Seven short days – and what a lot has happened. Seven hundred and sixty-three thousand babies have been born in China; two hundred and ninety-six million cups of tea have been drunk in the Northern Hemisphere alone; and two MPs, a bishop and a rock 'n' roll star have called British bird baths a national disgrace. The coast of Pembrokeshire has moved two millimetres nearer to the Azores; and for the eighty-first consecutive year, oil has been voted the most popular lubricant for sewing machines. This will give you an idea of the kind of week it has been beyond the shadows of Paddington Station. I must admit that *within* the shadows of Paddington Station life has been equally confused and meaningless. Mr Worth and me are still at Miss Boot's repulsive boarding house. As a matter of fact, we did make an attempt to shake the dust off our feet – but alas, owing to … well, I'll tell you exactly what happened …
GRAMS:	*Music link*
FX:	*Floorboards creaking*

MISS BOOT: (IRENE HANDL)	Time you were having your delicious brekkers. You know my rule about breakfast being from seven to seven-ten. Well – you've two minutes left.
FX:	*Door opens*
WORTH: (HARRY W)	What a picture! It looks like a winter landscape. The blackened stumps of the toast silhouetted against the grey of the tablecloth and, here and there, the muffled figure of an egg in its cosy.
DUDLEY:	Yes, and by the feel of it, Jack Frost has laid his icy hand on the teapot. Hello, Major, you're too late for breakfast – lucky devil.
MAJOR: (DICK EMERY)	I'm too excited to eat – I've been waiting for this letter for some time.
DUDLEY:	If you don't mind my asking, what's the letter about?
MAJOR:	It's in connection with the regimental dinner. We always have one at this time of year. I wouldn't miss it for the world. 'Course, a chap's got to keep up a certain style at this sort of function. That's why I've been making all kinds of little economies.
DUDLEY:	Yes, I noticed you were only taking one spoonful of curry powder in your tea.

There had been a previous series of *We're In Business*, the basic plot of which was Harry Worth being conned by Peter Jones in the character he'd first created with Peter Ustinov in the series *In All Directions*, Dudley Grosvenor. Charles Maxwell hadn't been too impressed by the scripts and brought Marty and me in because he'd liked what we were doing with the Glums in *Take It From Here*. Irene Handl played the landlady of the digs where Peter and Harry stayed, and Dick Emery played various roles, mainly the Major.

It worked quite well, was enjoyed by those who heard it, but never attracted a great audience and was dropped after two series.

Two incidents stand out. Irene Handl had the alarming habit of changing her dialogue, when the original displeased her, with an ancient fountain-pen using blue-black ink. Scripts are typed on fairly absorbent paper and the ink spread, obscuring not only the original but also her amendments. We would often have to wait for some time during the recording while she deciphered her scribbled alterations.

One day halfway through the series, during a break in rehearsal, she called Marty and me over and said in a voice tinged with sorrow and disappointment, 'You boys don't believe in the Bible.' Thinking we'd been unintentionally guilty of some piece of blasphemy, we asked what was the problem. Irene Handl said, 'Well, it says in the Bible that man and woman were created equal – and you've given Harry Worth more lines than you've given me'!

On another occasion Harry Worth had some trouble.

He said, 'Can I say this word? Isn't it rude?'

We asked what the word was.

He said, 'Here – look – *candlebra*.'

We explained that it wasn't a female undergarment but a light fitting, and told him how the word was pronounced.

'Oh,' he said 'I see!'

*

Marty and I did our television scriptwriting without outside help and it soon became obvious that we were bringing a new element to *The Army Game*. Actually the first person it became obvious to was Philip Purser, then the tv critic of the *News Chronicle*. He saw clearly what Marty and I had suspected, that the character played by Alfie Bass, 'Excused Boots' Bisley, better known as Bootsie, and that of Sergeant-Major Claude Snudge, played by Bill Fraser, were more than the cardboard cut-outs the earlier scripts sometimes suggested, and that beneath the khaki exteriors beat fierce passions. I'm not suggesting anything sexual but a relationship based on one individual's need for the other: for Bootsie a figure of authority to hate and mock, and for Snudge a creature demonstrably inferior over whom he held power.

It was another variation of the Hancock/Sid James relationship, and of *Steptoe and Son* which came some time later. It's the sort of relationship that held *The Likely Lads* together and made the battle of wits between prisoner Fletcher (Ronnie Barker) and warder Mr McKay (Fulton McKay) in *Porridge* so effective. The female equivalent is, I suppose, the various relationships developed in *The Liver Birds*; but anyway back in 1960, Granada Television in the persons of Cecil Bernstein and Denis Forman, not to mention producer Peter Eton, thought it would be a good idea to syphon Bootsie and Snudge off and give them their own series.

The main problem in finding a new situation for Bootsie and Snudge was that while they were in the Army the same set of rules governed them both, and both were bound by them. They could avoid them or get round them, but ultimately their actions were controlled by the greater authority of the Army.

In civilian life that authority doesn't exist and while the Army chained them together, civvy street freed them. Why then, we asked, should these two men, complete opposites in character and temperament, stay together? The answer was to put them into a civilian milieu where a pecking order similar to the Army existed.

We discussed and rejected the Police, the Fire Service, British Rail and the Foreign Legion. Eventually Peter Eton suggested that a good location would be a Pall Mall Club where Snudge could be the hall porter and Bootsie the handyman. We immediately saw the possibilities: an upstairs-downstairs situation (which pre-dated that excellent series by a decade) with the servants' quarters contrasted with the leather and mahogany atmosphere of the club proper.

We set to work and invented an ancient waiter (Clive Dunn), a senile old twit who thought that Snudge was General Kitchener magically restored to life, and the club secretary (Robert Dorning) who had to cope not only with the vagaries of the club members but with the oddities of his staff.

A series of thirty-nine programmes was planned, and when we complained that we couldn't possibly tackle that amount of work John Antrobus was added to the team to write a third of the scripts. I think in the end he only wrote three, of which two were unmemorable (for me anyway) and the third, called 'The Day Off', similar in some respects to the famous *Hancock's Half Hour* study of the boring Sunday, was very good indeed.

The way Marty and I began a script was to ask ourselves what *emotion* we were going to explore – anger, jealousy, lust, fear? Once that was decided, we'd discuss how the various characters fitted into the general thesis.

For instance, in one plot we had an old school friend of Snudge turn up at the club as a new member. Snudge is mortified that his old chum is prosperous while he is a humble servant. It turns out that the man is a confidence trickster and rogue, so Snudge's *amour propre* is restored.

In another story it is revealed that Snudge has a phobic fear of moths; in another Old Johnson the waiter is lured into matrimony but saved on the steps of the church by the revelation that the predatory woman is already married. In yet another story Alfie Bass, as Bootsie, restores a concert pianist's confidence when the old maestro fears that his memory has gone and that a forthcoming recital will be a disaster.

As the series progressed it became almost unbelievably popular, so much so that when after several weeks as top of the top ten in the ratings it dropped to third Granada summoned a crisis meeting to discover what was going wrong!

When analysed, it turned out that two things were wrong with the series. The first was that owing to a long opening credit sequence there wasn't enough time for the script to establish that week's plot in a more than perfunctory way; and second, and most important, we weren't building enough suspense in the scene leading up to the commercial break which would make the viewer stay tuned in order to see what would occur.

Cutting the opening titles gave us an extra minute of scene-setting, and heightening the drama as we went into the commercials (e.g. Bootsie being given the sack, or the Club being raided by the police, or, in one instance, one of the characters apparently drowning in the fog-enshrouded Thames) solved the problems, and in a fortnight's time we were back at number one.

On the writing side problems were emerging. Marty, whether because of his own temperament or because of the prompting of friends and relatives (I fancy it was a combination of the two) decided he'd had enough of what he described as my dictatorial attitude to the way the scripts were written and announced that he wanted to go it alone. To show the world that he was a genuine, serious writer he bought himself a black polo-neck sweater and a black leather jacket. This was after all 1960–61 and that was what the existentialists and other French intellectuals wore, and Marty wanted to prove that he was like them.

Left holding the *Bootsie and Snudge* baby, I got help from Bill Craig and the writing duo David Cumming and Derek Collyer. I also brought two other writers into the camp – Peter Miller and James Kelly, whose big tv success had been the Associated Rediffusion comedy starring Leslie Phillips, *Our Man at St Marks*. Between us all, plus contributions from other sources, we managed to weather the unilateral Marty Feldman storm.

After a while he dropped the 'alone I will face the world and prove to it my genius' stance, we got together again and wrote the special brand of oddball comedy that was our stock in trade. All through our working lives Marty would, from time to time, work himself into a state over some imagined slight. On one occasion he became peeved that I always answered the phone. I pointed out that as we were working in my home it was only natural that I should answer my own telephone.

On another occasion he complained bitterly because my name came first in our billing. It didn't worry me in the slightest and after that we were billed as Marty Feldman and Barry Took, to my entire satisfaction.

Back in the early sixties at Granada Marty's behaviour became increasingly eccentric and he claimed he could only work with jazz music playing, or at night when completely alone. This manic attitude came mercifully after we had completed the first series of *Bootsie and Snudge* and before we had started the second. It soon became apparent that Marty was deeply disturbed and at last, and almost too late, his wife Lauretta sent for the doctor who immediately diagnosed a severe hyperthyroid condition. Marty was taken into hospital that night and operated on the next day. The (almost total) removal of his over-active thyroid gland, the cause of his dementia, brought him back to normal and after a period of convalescence we started work again. But as a result of his condition his eyes bulged for the rest of his life. When he became a star in his own right in *Marty* and *The Marty Feldman Comedy Machine* for tv, and *Young Frankenstein* and *Silent Movie* for the cinema, he owed much to his appearance – the pop-eyed look for which he'll always be remembered.

The second series of *Bootsie and Snudge* was blighted by an actors' strike. The ruling was that only the actors under long-term contract could perform, and that meant that we had Bass, Fraser, Dorning and Dunn and no one else. At first the problem was not too bad as there were a number of situations in which no outsiders were required and we wrote episodes where they were locked in the washroom, marooned on a train in a railway siding, locked out of the club, and so on.

After a time, however, it became quite a strain on both actors and writers to keep up the pretence of a world inhabited by only four people. Mercifully the strike was at last settled, and to celebrate we wrote a parody of the Hitchcock film *Rear Window* in which (in the original) James Stewart, incapacitated in a race-track accident, sees a murder take place in the apartment block opposite his bedroom. No one believes him, but the murderer realises that he's been spotted and …

The film was a very effective spine-chiller, and for our version a special set of four apartments was built in the confines of the Chelsea studio. Bootsie and Snudge's room (which to give the impression of distance was built as far back as was possible, right under the audience seating in the old theatre's balcony) echoed the original to perfection. There was, of course, no murder and the incapacitated Snudge had imagined it all, but we were able to use eighteen actors, a great relief to us after the long strike if not altogether to the liking of Granada who had to pay them.

Although Marty came and went during the hundred episodes of *Bootsie and Snudge* that were finally made, the last thirteen being called *Foreign Affairs* and set in a British Embassy in the Middle East, the scripts that he and I wrote together were by far the best. We explored the relationships of all four of the principal actors in the series and had the pleasure of bringing in excellent actors in supporting roles.

The names I recall with most pleasure of all the people we used were Patricia Hayes, Honor Blackman, Warren Mitchell (in a variety of roles from an Italian hairdresser to an aged concert pianist) and Geoffrey Palmer who, in those days before he'd established himself, was usually cast as a policeman. In the first three series (eighty-seven programmes) the show was never out of the top ten and in its entire life (although it must be admitted that the last series was pretty ropey) it was never out of the top twenty.

One episode which I wrote solo had, through various contrivances, Alfie Bass as Bootsie talking face-to-face with Nikita Kruschev (played by the Australian actor Kenneth J. Warren). Although the series was basically broad comedy we never shied away from issues of the day, and when Marty left for good and I was writing day and night to satisfy the insatiable demands of a weekly schedule I feel that the standard remained high.

Bill Fraser, an actor of the old school, always knew his lines by the second day of rehearsal, while Alfie Bass would never be entirely word perfect until the dress rehearsal and often not always then.

The opposite nature of the characters they played was echoed in real life, Alfie Bass being extremely left-wing in his politics and Bill Fraser as far right as you could go. Bill rarely quibbled about the script. There it was – he learned it, acted it and went home. He wasn't bland though, and at one time conceived a great dislike of Clive Dunn who he thought, probably with justification, was upstaging him.

In a remarkable outburst one day he shouted 'I'm not feeding that b – – – – –' and stormed out of the rehearsal room. Until he'd simmered down Peter Eton asked me to write episodes in which Bill Fraser and Clive Dunn didn't meet.

After two or possibly three episodes where I kept them apart in the script and where the rehearsals took on a surreal quality with two actors rehearsing at one end of the room and the other two at the other end, Bill's anger eventually died down and normal service was resumed.

There was another period when we abandoned the Club and wrote six episodes where Alfie and Bill were on their own. I think they were well written and certainly well produced and directed (the director was Derek Bennett, better known for his drama work), but the Club setting and the character comedy supplied by Clive Dunn and Robert Dorning was what had helped make the show the success it had become and we went back to the old formula, with a certain amount of regret but with the knowledge that that was what the public (and of course Granada Television) wanted.

*

During this period Marty and I started writing for Frankie Howerd. Frankie, from being an overnight success in *Variety Bandbox* in the 1940s, had matured into a solid top-of-the-bill attraction on the music-hall circuit and in West End shows. He then played Bottom in an Old Vic production of *A Midsummer Night's Dream*, and went onto a tv series that was deeply unfunny, and in consequence his popularity waned.

I'd appeared with Frankie Howerd on several variety bills and we'd become good friends. When his popularity declined he, naturally enough, became very anxious and we'd often walk the streets of Holland Park, where he lived, for hours, discussing his problems. I even wrote some material for a summer season for him but, most important, he was welcomed in my home in Creighton Avenue, Muswell Hill and Dot cooked him many excellent dinners.

When Marty and I started to work together, Marty was intrigued with the idea of writing for Frankie, and thanks to BBC Radio producer Bill Worsley we were commissioned to write several scripts for him. When we delivered the first one Frankie read it and then said, 'Yes – not bad. But where are all the oohs and aahs?' His style, of course, was a well simulated impression of a clumsy, scatterbrained amateur. We said 'But surely you ad lib all those.' Frankie said 'Oh no. The writers have to put them in.' So we took the script back and added the various asides such as Frankie's catchphrases 'Chilly', 'What a funny woman', 'I'm laughing and I'm in it', and the oohs and aahs that were asked for and for which Frankie was known. From then on we wrote all the ad libs in and Frankie delivered them as if they'd entered his head at that moment.

The great trick of writing comedy for people is to understand their style and if necessary imitate it, a fact which Marty and I learned very quickly in our career.

Writing one-off scripts for radio comedians was always a meagrely paid enterprise. We agreed a fee with Frankie for £20 a script and after the first one had been accepted and broadcast we shyly mentioned the financial arrangement. Frankie said to me, 'You don't need money! Look, I've got this set of *Encyclopaedia Britannica*. You take it in payment and give Marty a tenner.'

Which is what I did. Marty got £10 and I got a set of encyclopaedias, which stare sombrely at me from my bookcase as I write this nearly thirty years later.

Marty and I subsequently wrote a series for Howerd called *Frankie's Bandbox*, and he was then taken up by Ned Sherrin in *That Was The Week That Was*, appeared in Peter Cook's Establishment Club and took on Johnny Speight as his writer. We remained friends, and are to this day.

During all these alarms and excursions, and every week seemed to produce its new crisis, I met and fell in love with Lyn. We ran away together and have lived together happily ever since: married, I need hardly add, for over twenty-five years.

8

New Wife, New Agent, New Work, New Life

In 1962 my home life with Dot was extremely miserable although a third child, David, had arrived, a delightful baby grown today into an amusing, athletic and thoroughly decent adult.

At the time I was on the verge of a long drawn out period of psychoanalysis. I had no idea what I was in for, but looking back I regard my four years 'on the couch' as a life-enhancing experience and, because of what I learnt, not only about myself but the world around me, it was the equivalent of the further education I never had.

My analyst was Hilda Abraham, daughter of the distinguished Berlin analyst Carl Abraham, a contemporary and friend of Sigmund Freud. Hilda Abraham had been analysed by Freud and was a Freudian in the true sense of the word. She really understood what Freud meant and used his methods thoroughly and effectively.

I wouldn't presume to say that I totally understood the process then, and I don't today, but I can say that, frightening and difficult though a thoroughly Freudian analysis might be, the insight that a successful analysis generates in the patient, the inner peace, the self-knowledge and the deeper understanding of life in all its aspects that it generates is worth every moment of fear, doubt and self-loathing that the patient feels en route to the conclusion of the treatment.

That it was a success in my case can be seen in the stability of my relationship with my wife, Lyn, whom I adore, and our daughter, Elinor, who is better educated, more intelligent and more gifted than either Lyn or I.

My working life since analysis has not been significantly more successful than my career before it, but I can say that I've enjoyed my work more and can cope with occasional bouts of self-doubt, jealousy and rancour in a reasonably adult and balanced way.

The cost of the analysis – and it is expensive – is in a way a part of the treatment, bringing up as it does the feelings of resentment from the patient – 'Why should I pay this person all this money for doing *nothing*!' It's often the first sort of resentment to surface and leads, in time, to other resentments both fiscal and sexual.

The main problems with psychoanalysis are that it's a long process, time-consuming and slow; I had four sessions a week for the four years of my treatment. Also, it's not effective in every case, and many people give up half way or before. But, from the patient's point of view, if you can stick with it, Freudian psychoanalysis can be – and certainly was in my case – a wonderful life-enhancing experience.

*

But let's get back to our story. A quick resumé is perhaps needed as you may have dozed off during the last few pages.

The year is 1963. I have left Granada and am living in what was once called 'Sin' in a two-bedroom flat near Regents Park, waiting for my divorce to become absolute.

Marty Feldman and I have resumed working together and are about to start what historically will be seen as our 'golden' period.

The way Marty and I got back together as a writing team is as follows. While I was still at Granada finishing off, in every sense of the phrase, *Bootsie and Snudge*, Marty, through his agent Kenneth Ewing of Fraser and Dunlop, had sold the BBC Light Entertainment department a series idea based on the adventures of two old men. Marty very much wanted to write a comedy of old age and it was generally thought to be a good idea. The title Marty had come up with was '*You're Only Old Once*', but having thought of these two old men sitting in a graveyard chatting he had become stuck.

He came to me with the problem and I can remember us walking round and round Golden Square trying to find a solution. It seemed to me that attractive though the idea was we needed to know more about the old men concerned. After all, chatting in a graveyard is one thing – but what are they going to chat *about*? By the time we'd finished our perambulations around the square we had devised the following: One of the old men was a retired schoolmaster – a housemaster at a public school, living in digs, a man who although extremely learned had never ventured out into the rough-and-tumble of the real world. The other old man was the opposite: an ex-merchant seaman who had been everywhere and seen everything but who had no formal education and was, to all intents and purposes, illiterate. He lived with his houseproud daughter who kicked him out every morning and only allowed him back at supper time.

These two old men, who were subsequently named Gascoigne Quilt (the ex-teacher), and Luther Flannery (the ex-merchant seaman), met on a bench in the graveyard when the weather was clement and in the church when it rained. Being poor and having nowhere to go their activities were restricted, but Luther Flannery's sense of adventure and Mr Quilt's eagerness to follow his new friend into activities he'd never have contemplated on his own gave the series its driving force.

The two men, each possessing qualities and abilities the other lacked, were never at a loss for conversation, and Marty and I, once the basis of the series had been laid down, had a great time writing the various episodes.

Here are two examples.

In the first they are in the Reading Room of the local library. Luther confesses he cannot read and Mr Quilt offers to read to him. They wander along the shelves of books, and Quilt points to one.

QUILT: How about the poems of Shelley?

LUTHER: No. It's only a thin little book. I want something that'll last. Like that –

Takes down a huge volume.

QUILT: The dictionary.

LUTHER: Yes. This is the one. There's all the words in the world here. Little fat short words, great long thin words, words with hyphens, words in brackets, words with capitals. Every word you could wish for. Read me this, Mr Quilt.

QUILT: But it'll take ages.

LUTHER: The longer the better. What's the hurry? We're not going anywhere.

They get the book back to the table during this.

QUILT: Well, if it's really what you want ...

LUTHER: It is, Mr Quilt. It is.

QUILT: Alright then ...

They sit. Quilt opens the book.

QUILT: (*Reads*) A.

LUTHER: (*Excited*) What does it say about it? What does it say about it?

QUILT: (*Reads*) A. Letter and noun. Sixth note in the scale of C Major. First known quantity. First hypothetical person. First class. First rate.

LUTHER: All that? One little letter means all that. It's a world in itself. (*Repeats it*) A. The sixth note in the scale of C Major. Who'd have thought it? Read on, Mr Quilt.

QUILT: Ab. Prefix. Away from.

LUTHER: (*Ecstatically happy now*) Oh, there's lovely. It's poetry.

QUILT: Abacus ... device with balls sliding on wires, used for calculating.

LUTHER: Abacus. Yes. Balls on wires. For calculating. Good, good. Next, Mr Quilt.

QUILT: Abandon. Give up, yield up, surrender, forsake, relinquish. Abandonment. Careless freedom ...

LUTHER: (*Beside himself with joy*) Abandonment. Careless freedom – oh, that's got a swagger to it, ennit? That's philosophy that is. (*Voice getting louder without realising it*) Freedom. Careless freedom, that's abandonment for you.

Librarian shushes them.

Luther subsides.

Quilt carries on in a low voice.

QUILT: Abase. Humiliate, lower – Abasement ... Abash ...

Fade

In this next extract the elderly couple are on their way to Wales to stay with an old friend of Luther's, Charlie Price.

They are hitch-hiking and have been dropped off at a transport café. They enter, and Quilt goes to the counter.

QUILT: Two teas please, mine host – and are your pork pies fresh?

PROPRIETOR: (*Sarcastically*) Course they're fresh. Them flies wouldn't hang about 'em if they wasn't. They're no mugs, flies. How many do you want?

QUILT: How much are they?

PROPRIETOR: One and three each.

QUILT: Oh. (*He crosses to table and consults with Luther. Much whispering and shaking of heads. He walks back sedately*) We'll have half a one.

PROPRIETOR: (*As he cuts one in half and slaps it on plate*) Oi – Albert! We got the Rothschilds in.

A lorry driver at the Juke Box, to whom this is addressed, laughs.

PROPRIETOR: (*Teapot poised*) How do you wannit?

QUILT: (*Carefully, as if explaining the theory of relativity to a backward child*) One with sugar, one without sugar. The one without sugar with milk and the one with sugar without milk. The milky one not too milky, but not too strong; say the colour of well-weathered mahogany ... The one without milk half filled and topped up with hot water. Shall I repeat that?

PROPRIETOR: (*Who has just been staring at him in disbelief*) No. No. That's alright. One thing – what colour would you like the cups?

He pours two mugs of tea and shoves them at Quilt who takes tea and pork pie to table where Luther sits. He joins him and looks sadly at the meal.

QUILT: They do this sort of thing so much better on the Continent.

Owing to my exclusive contract with Granada at the time I couldn't take a credit on the BBC pilot script – subsequently the first episode – but by the time a series of six programmes was commissioned I had left Granada and was once again a freelance. For the sake of convenience and because I admired his skill as a literary agent, I joined Marty as a client of Kenneth

Ewing. Kenneth and his assistant, Jill Foster (who now runs her own successful company), were very good at handling both would-be employers and their own clients, who could at times be extremely tricky. Many writers, like most actors, are sensitive souls, need constant reassurance, are jealous of their competitors and constantly suspect that the agent is not doing enough for them. My own view is that the agent is as good as the writer (or actor) he or she represents and that the talented will always work whoever looks after the business.

The title *The Walrus and the Carpenter*, as the two-old-men series was finally called, was the invention of the actor Felix Aylmer who played the retired schoolmaster. Hugh Griffith, the Welsh Shakespearean actor, played Flannery.

The scripts were read with great enjoyment by the BBC's Light Entertainment bosses and were generally supposed at the time to be excellent pieces of writing, which perhaps they were.

When the series went on the air the reviews were flattering. Richard Sear wrote in the *Daily Mirror*:

> Nothing like this comedy has been written for television and few comedies have brought together such a superb combination of actors as Felix Aylmer and Hugh Griffith. The humour is mature and detached.

Norman Hare wrote in the *Daily Telegraph*:

> Marty Feldman and Barry Took have brought to the screen a delightful old couple whose ramblings provide much amusement.

and Adrian Mitchell, writing in the pre-Murdoch *Sun*, who incidentally reviewed the series on more than one occasion, said of the third episode:

> To those who like their tv slick, flawless and forgettable I would never recommend *The Walrus and the Carpenter*. But for those who like rough edges, eccentricity and a touch of senile delinquency the series is irresistible.

Felix Aylmer was a quick learner and had the endearing habit of calling each episode 'this week's play'. He was also hot on continuity and if he spotted an inconsistency in his character he would take it up with us during rehearsals.

Hugh Griffith, larger than life both on and off stage, was a heavy drinker and this tended to slow down his delivery. So much so that one episode nearly ground to a halt so slow did it become.

Tom Sloan, who was the BBC TV Head of Light Entertainment, thought that to teach him a lesson he would call Hugh Griffith in and play a recording of the episode, at which Griffith would smite his forehead, realise the error of his ways, apologise and speed up his delivery in future. The screening was duly set up and Griffith ensconced in front of the tv set in Sloan's office. The episode dragged its weary length and at the finish Sloan said, 'Well, Hugh?' Griffith replied 'Very good. Excellent. I see nothing the matter with that at all.' He was a wily, amusing, frustrating old mountebank of whom we all became extremely fond even when, after he had sworn to give up hard liquor and drink Coca Cola instead, it was noticed that the Coke he drank gave off an almost overpowering smell of rum.

Although the critics received *The Walrus and the Carpenter* very well, the public didn't care for it and viewing figures were poor. The producer, James Gilbert, Marty and I were discussing this problem and how to solve it in the second series which had been mooted when Tom Sloan strode into Gilbert's office and said bluntly, 'Well, what went wrong?' As I have indicated, writers can be sensitive beings and we were deeply irritated by this brusque, philistine approach. Our reaction was to say well, if it was wrong let's forget it, which we did and no more were made.

My own feeling is that the sight of two old men, however amusing, living out their few remaining years was rather depressing, because after all the only outcome could have been their deaths.

Years later when a very good script with a similar theme arrived at the BBC, I pointed out the problems we'd had with *Walrus* and suggested that the three elderly retired men in the script should be rewritten as much younger: one as a recently retired army man in his fifties, one made redundant, and the third unemployable. That way their end wasn't inevitable as they could all get jobs, remarry and in many ways change their lives. The fact that they didn't would be immaterial but the possibility was there. I also suggested a change of location from

Doncaster, where the writer had set it, to Holmfirth where I'd recently made a documentary and which I thought would be an ideal setting. The series was, of course, *The Last of the Summer Wine*, beautifully written by Roy Clarke, which starred (originally) Michael Bates and later Brian Wilde and Michael Aldridge, plus the ever-present Peter Sallis, and Bill Owen as the revolting Compo.

The next television writing that Marty and I did was a number of 'one offs' in the Comedy Playhouse series. (Comedy Playhouse was a series of unconnected programmes – a testing ground for new ideas.)

Our imagination ran riot, especially in our titles. There was *Barnaby Spoot and the Exploding Whoopee Cushion*, which starred John Bird and was produced by Dick Clement (co-creator with Ian la Frenais of *The Likely Lads*). The story was of an assistant in a joke and novelty shop whose creative urges are constantly frustrated. For instance, he invents a talking cheese, 'I am chatty cheddar, pleased to meet you', which is rejected by the board of directors and as a result (it goes without saying that Barnaby Spoot is round the bend) he decides to blow them up by inventing an exploding whoopee cushion. (A whoopee cushion is a rubber balloon which when blown up and then sat upon makes an extremely rude and embarrassing sound.)

The eponymous hero has a change of heart and the episode ends on an up-beat note, but it was original and amusing and John Bird was extremely good as Spoot. Our next venture was called *Memoirs of a Chaise Longue*. A popular film of the time was *The Yellow Rolls Royce*, a trio of stories in contrasting styles in which the Rolls Royce figured. We thought, why not a similar trio of stories centred on a more mundane object? Our first thought was a commode, an idea we rapidly rejected, but after some discussion we agreed that a chaise longue would be ideal and that its story could be told by an actor's face (ideally Kenneth Williams) superimposed on an ornamental scroll on the chaise longue. The part was in fact played by Alan Melville. The stories were respectively elegant, sinister and farcical.

The first story, set in the 1890s, was a pastiche in the manner of an Oscar Wilde play with a touch of Parisian Boulevard comedy thrown in. The protagonists were two married couples, each wife being the mistress of the other man. It is revealed that they actually are in love with their husbands and all ends happily and morally.

The second story, set in Sidcup, was played with great skill by John Le Mesurier and Betty Marsden, and concerned a much married, and as often widowed, woman. The period was the thirties, and as they sat on the chaise longue the widow told her suitor about her previous husbands and how she engineered their death always seemingly at the hands of their successor, her next husband. The suitor (John Le Mesurier) realises that he too has been used and incriminated and that he must marry the predatory widow. It was black comedy lightened by descriptions of the strange occupations of the widow's former husbands and the manner of their death. For instance, one was a taxidermist who died while tattooing himself with a loyal slogan (a poisoned tattooing needle being the murder weapon): 'He died in mid tattoo, with "God save the Quee" on his chest. I often wonder what the Almighty made of that.' Another victim, a haberdasher, apparently hanged himself with a pair of braces 'with doggie's heads on them. He never had no taste'.

As you can see, not a jolly surburban romp.

The last episode concerned an Irish wedding in Kilburn, where the two families – the Mooleys and the Poltroons, sworn enemies since the 1916 Revolution, are briefly united by young Bridget Mooley and Kevin Poltroon, who had consummated their passion on the chaise longue and in consequence had to marry rather hurriedly. During the wedding breakfast old grievances are aired, old scores are settled by the two rival families, and the whole episode ends in a massive fist fight.

I honestly believe that it was one of the cleverest pieces of work Marty and I ever did together, elegantly constructed and very funny.

Two other scripts we wrote at that time, *Tooth and Claw*, a story of two rival millionaires, and *The Making of Peregrine* about a father's worry that his son was effeminate, were shelved but made later, with Warren Mitchell and Marty Feldman playing Tooth and Claw, and Dick Emery and Andrew Ray starring in Peregrine. Neither was terribly successful and showed the BBC's wisdom in shelving them.

Our next series starred Irene Handl and Bill Fraser and was called *Barney is my Darling*. The producer was again James Gilbert, and although it should have been a reasonable success the 'chemistry' never happened and it was, to be frank, a damp squib which everyone connected with it quickly forgot. Literally so in my case as many years later passing an off-licence called Brown and Pank I said to Marty, 'Didn't we once write something about a man called Pank?' We racked our brains and at last dredged up *Barney is my Darling*. Barney's surname had been Pank.

The plot wasn't that bad. The idea was that many years before the action started a steward on an ocean liner (Barney Pank) had married a hairdresser's assistant and on their honeymoon a son had been conceived. Then the steward went to sea, to the China Seas to be precise, and apart from one or two fleeting meetings in the interim the couple, although married, hadn't met for over twenty years.

On his retirement the steward comes home expecting it to have remained unchanged but of course everything is different. His wife now owns the hairdressing salon and is a busy business woman, and her pet dog (in our original script a large, ageing, scruffy mongrel) sleeps on her bed and resents Barney's presence. The son is in prison and, taking one consideration with another, as the song has it, Barney's lot is not a happy one.

It could have worked but it didn't, but by then our eyes were set on other targets. A series planned for Kenneth Williams was in fact made with Terry Scott when Williams backed out. We wrote three scripts: *Scott on Birds* (a mock documentary on the subject of women), *Scott on Money* and *Scott on Food*. I seem to remember we subtitled them 'World in Acton' and the style was a direct parody of the investigative tv journalism of the time exemplified by *World in Action, This Week* and *Panorama*. Later the BBC used our title 'Scott on' for a long series starring Terry Scott, but we were only concerned with the first three.

I remember some sketches from our *Scott on* programmes as being near-classics of the sketch form. In one Terry played a male Playboy Bunny in the fishnet stockings, satin bodice and fluffy white ears and tail. 'You can look at me and talk to me, but you can't touch me' he tells a couple of prurient business women. In another Terry was a mother-dominated middle-aged man still in the rompers and ringlets of childhood. Marty revived and played in both these sketches in his own series some time later. Then there was a sketch we called 'Rich Prejudice' which treated the rich then moving into the hitherto working-class areas of Islington and Highbury as a racist would have treated coloured immigrants.

> 'They have all-night parties with music blaring away … and their food is different to ours …' (says Terry Scott as a helmeted 'Biker') 'caviar, pâté de foie gras, and little curly cucumbers … and they smell different. I wouldn't mind going with one of their women but I wouldn't want my sister marrying one …' etc.

There was a parody of *Goldfinger*, called Fishfinger, set in Billingsgate, and a lot more goodies, including Harry Carpenter commentating on an eating contest. The commentary had been prerecorded, but Harry and his wife were in the studio audience for the rest of the recording. As was fairly common in those days there was a technical breakdown which went on and on and after I'd chatted to the audience for what seemed an eternity I invited Harry Carpenter onto the studio floor to talk about his recent trip to America and his commentary on the historic first Sonny Liston/Cassius Clay fight. Harry was spell-binding and I think the audience was sorry when the recording of *Scott on Food* resumed.

*

By now Marty and I were really busy, and my filing system reveals that from 1959 to 1965 we wrote, apart from the shows already mentioned, a one-off for Rediffusion called *Climping of the Titanic*, about adjoining cinemas which like the ship in the title sank in the icy waters of Rediffusion's comedy department; and two episodes of a series for Granada, *A Little Big Business*, based on an idea of mine called Heart of Gold, and written by Jack Pulman. The series was about a furniture manufacturer and his go-ahead son, played by David Kossoff and Francis Matthews. The episodes written by Marty and me were called 'The Bespoke Coffin' and 'I'll Take a Knighthood if the Price is

Right'. They were paid for but never used. Others still gathering dust in a cupboard somewhere were 'The World of Dudley Grosvenor' (for Peter Jones), 'Wilkie', a radio script for Clive Dunn, 'Off the Rails', written for Robert Dorning and Clive Dunn, and 'Tea at the Ritz' directed by Graeme McDonald, a not dissimilar comedy to the film *The Smallest Show on Earth*, both scripted by me solo. I also wrote (with David Cumming) a number of radio sketches for Lance Percival and Patsy Rowlands in a series called *Showtime '63*, and a series of thirteen radio sit-coms, also with David Cumming, called *Two Plus Two* which starred Barbara Windsor, Anton Rogers, Lance Percival and Patsy Rowlands, with Arthur Howard and later Derek Nimmo as the local vicar.

At around that time Marty and I were commissioned by Betty Box to write the screenplay for a film called *The Red Hot Ferrari* for which we were handsomely paid but which, for one reason or another, was never made.

The Red Hot Ferrari had begun to take shape in my mind years before when I was told a (true) story by the trumpet player in the Steve Race band on *Late Extra*. It went like this: A man goes on holiday to Rimini. He's not well off but is looking for some Italian sun. Every day he is pestered by the local lottery seller and after refusing to buy for some time, eventually, to get rid of this pest, buys one ticket for a hundred lire.

It turns out that he has the winning ticket and the prize is a Fiat car. He has come to Italy by air and already has a car in England. So, he sells the Fiat, crams the millions of lire into his suitcase and departs for the airport.

Meanwhile a poor Italian widow wants desperately to win the car for her son who could then become a travelling salesman. To make ends meet she works in a restaurant in Rimini during the summer and in a London hotel as a chambermaid in the winter. She has bought lottery tickets containing every permutation of every lucky number that her superstition suggests and prayed to every saint in the calendar. Now, as she sits in the Heathrow-bound Alitalia aeroplane, two seats behind the 'lucky Inglese', her rage at the capriciousness of fate wells up. At Heathrow the unsuspecting Englishman is about to walk through the 'nothing to declare' section of customs when the

Italian woman screeches out, 'That man has a suitcase stuffed with millions of lire!'

At that time it was illegal to export or import large sums of money unless one was licensed to do so. The customs man beckons, the suitcase is opened, the money is confiscated and the luckless Inglese is heavily fined. All for the sake of a one hundred lire lottery ticket.

By making the venue Sicily and the car a Ferrari, and rewriting the widow as the entire Sicilian Mafia, the story reached cinematic proportions and developed into a hectic chase across Europe. Betty Box still calls it 'the best screenplay that was never made'.

But amidst this welter of failure and forgettability one piece of work stood out, for in 1965 we were asked to write the show that became *Round the Horne*.

9

Round the Horne

There are few radio shows that could be said to be truly innovative. The Goons broke new ground, as did *I'm Sorry I'll Read That Again, I'm Sorry I Haven't A Clue* and *Hitchhiker's Guide to the Galaxy*. In passing it should be noted that television lagged behind radio but came good in the early sixties with *That Was The Week That Was, Not So Much A Programme More A Way Of Life*, and *BBC 3* (all Ned Sherrin productions), and later *Till Death Us Do Part, Marty, Monty Python's Flying Circus* and *Not the Nine O'Clock News*.

Round the Horne back in 1965 was certainly innovative, our targets being not so much the political as the sexual and moral, or should I say immoral, attitudes of the time (Vassall, Burgess and Maclean, and Kim Philby come to mind). When Marty and I were first asked to write a replacement for the long-running and successful *Beyond Our Ken*, which Eric Merriman had carried on with help from various sources, not least from Kenneth Horne himself, for some years after my departure, we were at first unwilling. The reason Merriman came to leave this lucrative and successful show is odd, and sadly typical of the man.

Kenneth Horne, who even when 'idle' was a busy man travelling all over the UK and appearing in a variety of radio and tv shows, was asked in 1964 to star in a radio comedy series *Down With Women* and duly made a pilot show. For some reason this irritated Merriman and he said to the BBC what amounted to 'If *Down With Women* is broadcast I will withdraw *Beyond Our Ken*'.

In a letter to the BBC in November 1964, Merriman wrote: 'I

note that you have decided to continue with your plans to broadcast *Down With Women*. Regretfully, therefore, I confirm that you must now consider that *Beyond Our Ken* is at an end.'

It was at this point that the BBC, not unreasonably, started to look around for other writers for a new series featuring the *Beyond Our Ken* team. Informing Merriman of this (and incidentally sounding out Marty Feldman and me as to whether we would take on the assignment) Roy Rich, who had taken over the job as Head of Light Entertainment from Pat Hillyard, received a reply from Merriman in a letter dated 30 November 1964 in which, in part, he says:

> I consider the piratical action you propose to take … highly unethical … in that you intend to reproduce the whole essence of an established show which I created and originally cast.

This was both unfair and untrue. When you consider that in the original cast of *Beyond Our Ken* three members, Hugh Paddick, Ron Moody and Pat Lancaster were colleagues of mine from the West End revue *For Adults Only* in which Merriman had no interest except as a member of the audience (we *had* written a sketch which was used briefly in the out-of-town tour but that had been dropped for the West End) and that Kenneth Williams had joined the team at the suggestion of Pat Hillyard, who as Head of Light Entertainment had commissioned the show in the first place, the claim to have 'created and cast' *Beyond Our Ken* is ludicrous.

A tentative title for the *Beyond Our Ken* replacement was *It's Ken Again*, and Merriman reacted in his letter as follows:

> I have taken note of your statement that this is to be 'a new programme with a new look' from which I assume that there is to be no infringement of format, features, characters, or the various devices which I employed to give the show its unique flavour … a proposed title whereby the use of 'Ken' and more particularly 'Again' is by inference a sequel to the original title … or in legal parlance 'passing off'.

When consulted on this point the then Head of BBC Copyright, R.G. Walford, in a memo to Roy Rich dated 3 December 1964 said:

> I see no objection to your title *It's Ken Again*, which in my view puts the emphasis on the actor Kenneth Horne rather than referring to the previous show, *Beyond Our Ken*.

On 14 December 1964 Roy Rich sent copies of all this correspondence to Marty and me with a covering letter saying, in part:

> I am sending them to you as a further affirmation (or proof if you prefer it) of my determination that *It's Ken Again* shall indeed be a new show. I have the greatest respect for your reluctance to perpetuate the old formula …

So far, so much a storm in a tea cup; but various important factors were involved. The 'reluctance' that Roy Rich mentions stemmed from the fact that at a meeting with Rich, Kenneth Horne, John Simmonds (the producer) and Edward Taylor (the Light Entertainment Script Editor) we had said no to the proposition that we should write the successor to *Beyond Our Ken*. Our main objection was that it had been running for years and that it would be difficult to find anything new for such an entrenched cast to perform.

Having thanked the BBC team for asking, we returned to my flat and had lunch. Marty, being a vegetarian, was something of a problem where food was concerned, but Lyn enjoyed her forays into vegetarian cookery as a change from her more usual Cordon Bleu style, and over lunch we discussed the BBC's proposition. Being of an inventive turn of mind we starting conjecturing what *could* be done with *Beyond Our Ken*, and by the time lunch was over we'd come up with so many ideas for Horne and his team that we phoned Roy Rich and, somewhat embarrassed, said that we'd changed our minds and would like to have a shot at a new series.

The pilot script was sufficiently encouraging for the BBC to proceed with a series, and in February 1965 we started work in earnest on the show I had now persuaded the BBC to call *Round the Horne*.

The cast responded nobly to what we gave them, never complained and certainly seemed to enjoy playing the new characters we created for them.

Our thinking was that as radio was no longer *the* popular entertainment form (by 1965 tv had become almost totally dominant) we had not only to delight but to surprise our audience, and as the gap between writing the script and its going on air was rarely more than ten days we felt able to be topical, using names from that week's news stories, passing on West End theatrical gossip and, with a subtle name change or two, lampooning the popular heroes of the day.

We had no idea that the shows would be broadcast, or indeed be broadcastable, after the obligatory repeats, and it is with a combination of amazement and delight that I record that twenty-five years later *Round the Horne* is still going strong, surprisingly avant-garde and even risqué, which perhaps shows that the 1990s are no more sophisticated than the 1960s.

If *Beyond Our Ken* was popular *Round the Horne* was a world-beater and can still be heard in many countries worldwide and not infrequently in the UK too, such is the demand for repeats of one of the most iconoclastic radio series ever made by the BBC.

Here are some examples. This was the opening to one programme in 1965.

KENNETH W:	Scream as much as you like, my dear. No one can hear you here.
BETTY:	But why have you strapped me to this operating table?
KENNETH W:	Call it an old man's whim.
BETTY:	All right, why have you strapped me to this old man's whim, and what are you doing with that little black box?
KENNETH W:	Don't worry, my dear, you won't feel a thing. I just attach a wire here, a wire there, then I turn this knob and ...
DOUGLAS:	This is the BBC. Ladies and gentlemen, it's *Round the Horne*.
BETTY:	No, no. Anything but that.

This was a sketch vintage 1966, written when Julian and Sandy had become great favourites with the audience:

KENNETH H:	I always thought that fox-hunting was the prerogative of the wealthy few, so was amazed when I saw an advertisement in my copy of *Peek-a-Boo Corset Pictorial* – I buy it for the spot-the-ball contest. The advertisement read: 'The Bona Hunt – Come trolling after the fox with us in specially selected groups.' It

sounded just what I wanted so I hurried over to the address in Carnaby Street as fast as my lallies would carry me.

KENNETH H: Hello. Anybody there?

HUGH: Oh hello. I'm Julian and this is my friend, Sandy.

KENNETH W: Oh, it's Mr Horne.

HUGH: Yoicks, Tally Ho, ducky!

KENNETH W: We are your actual Carnaby Hunt. Jule's MFH. I'm the Whipper in.

KENNETH H: And very nice you look too. How many of you are there in the hunt?

HUGH: Just Sandy and me so far.

KENNETH W: And of course Reynard.

KENNETH H: The Fox?

KENNETH W: No ducky. Reynard La Spoon, the choreographer – he's a close personal, ent he, Jule?

HUGH: An intime – you'll get on well with him. He's your type – all butch.

KENNETH W: But questing. You must have seen his work. He does fantastic things on the television.

HUGH: You know, they all come trolling on in form-hugging black and do evocative things with chairs and ladders and planks of wood. He once done something with a bentwood chair that made Robert Helpmann's eyes stand out like organ stops.

KENNETH W: It was his own fault for standing so close. Course, Reynard's classical trained –

HUGH: Oh yes. He's got your full classical.

KENNETH W: Started in John Cranko's *Nutcracker* and worked his way up.

HUGH: He supported Dame Margot's *Sleeping Beauty* when Nureyev backed out.

KENNETH H: And he's the only other member of the hunt, is he?

KENNETH W: So far – but we're hoping to attract your show business clientele.

KENNETH H: And where do you hunt from?

HUGH: Oh here – in Carnaby Street.

KENNETH H: There can't be many foxes in Carnaby Street.

HUGH: No. Not foxes. There's not what you could call a

plethora of foxes round here, but you still have the thrill of the chase.

KENNETH H: The chase? But what can you find to chase in Carnaby Street?

KENNETH W: He's very jejeune, isn't he, Jule?

HUGH: It's a quality I admire in him. Would that I still had it. Où sont les neiges d'antan, Mr Horne?

KENNETH W: That's your actual philosophical French. Still, don't brood, Jule, you'll get lines.

HUGH: Now Mr Horne, you ready for the off? Just put this pink coat on, and these breeches.

KENNETH W: And these bijou bootettes.

KENNETH H: What happens now?

KENNETH W: We just wait here till we vada the quarry. Look, there he goes – after him!

KENNETH H: But what about the horse?

KENNETH W: What horse? Jump on Jule's back.

KENNETH H: We chased the ginger furry creature down the road. Unfortunately it turned out to be Mick Jagger in a fun fur. He went to earth in a gents' boutique calling itself the Gay Hussar – and I didn't have the nerve to go in after him.

One of Marty and my favourite characters was the seedy, eccentric J. Peasemold Gruntfuttock, who popped up in the most unlikely situations:

KENNETH H: This week the Colour Supplement turns its bleary eye on the subject of the BBC radio – the elephants' graveyard of entertainment. To be fair, the BBC are always searching for new talent – take the script department.

HUGH: So you're our new scriptwriter, Mr …

KENNETH W: Gruntfuttock: J. Peasemold Gruntfuttock.

HUGH: Well, well, well – er – welcome aboard. Now I've been looking at some of the scripts you've sent in and, well I know you're new at it but – er – there are limits. I mean, look at the synopsis you sent in for the Dales. The incident you envisage in the bathroom between Mrs Dale, Bomber Harris, and Dr Adam York concerning the loofah, the mirror on a stick and the inflatable rubber duck – whilst not without its dramatic highlights, it would, I should think, be extremely dangerous to all concerned.

KENNETH W: Not at all. I tried it out. The loofah snapped but the rubber duck come through it unscathed.

HUGH: What about this scene? You can't have Mrs Dale and Mrs Freeman crouched on a bomb site swigging meths.

KENNETH W: That's the trouble with you lot. You're stuffy and hidebound. You don't want the fresh clean wind of reality blowing up your corridors of power.

HUGH: But look at this dialogue –

KENNETH W: Let me read it to you. You'll get the full flavour of it then. 'Enter Mrs Dale in her flimsy night attire, her bronzed young ...'

HUGH: Yes, quite. We can skip the stage directions.

KENNETH W: Mrs Dale speaks. 'Why hello, Jim – Cor, stone me, what a booze up we had last night up the BMA. My mouth's like the bottom of a parrot's cage.' To which her better half replies: 'Shut up you silly old tart or I'll give you a mouthful of knuckles.' There – what's wrong with that?

HUGH: It hasn't quite the nuance we expect. It just won't do, Mr Gruntfuttock. Your work is obviously the product of a one-track degenerate childish mind.

KENNETH W: I suppose that means you're giving me the sack?

HUGH: Good heavens, no. You're just the chap we need to write *Round the Horne*.

Many people have asked me why *Round the Horne* still sounds fresh and still holds an audience. I don't think that there is any one answer, but primarily it was unselfconscious. Oh, I know that a lot of it was taken up by the alleged 'internal wranglings' where Kenneth Williams would complain that he wasn't being serviced, but it was written to no set of rules, very quickly (two short days' work was the average) and moved from idea to idea as the ideas struck us. It was never a case of one writing the plots, the other the jokes. The scripts, all our scripts, were written jointly with us sitting side by side at a desk and me writing in longhand. Lyn would subsequently type the script and was always the first to read it, frequently amazed at the bizarre situations we had created.

Once agreed on a sketch or routine, Marty and I wrote very quickly. The important part of our working day was the gossip which preceded the actual writing. This might start with a discussion of, say, the previous night's football match or theatre visit, what we'd seen on tv or the books we were currently reading. We'd drink coffee and smoke cigarettes, and as the adrenaline started to flow so too would the ideas. Actually, Marty claimed that we didn't write the scripts but that they were created by an unseen presence called Marty Took or Barry Feldman. Such was our rapport I don't think he was far wrong.

The cast of *Round the Horne* were a great stimulus, each with their own characteristics and idiosyncrasies which we noted and used. Bill Pertwee lived on the South Coast and complained that he had to get up so early he caught the workmen's train. From that we imagined him as a nineteenth-century navvy with string tied round his trousers, smoking a clay pipe, and with his lunch in a red spotted handkerchief.

Kenneth Williams was always full of anecdotes of working with such stars as Alec Guinness and Dame Edith Evans. The former it seems was furious with Williams during the run of *Hotel Paradiso* for making an entrance with his trousers unbuttoned, believing that Williams had done it to get an extra laugh. Kenneth denied it, but the ribald streak in his nature must have made Guinness see it as a possibility. The story Williams told about Dame Edith concerned them on tour in a play called *Gentle Jack*.

Staying at the same hotel but getting there somewhat later than Dame Edith, Kenneth was greeted by the aged waiter saying to him, 'Good evening, sir. Your partner in crime is already in the dining-room.' The thought of the aristocratic Dame Edith Evans being described as 'your partner in crime' struck Kenneth as hilarious.

Naturally when he told these anecdotes Williams adopted a variety of accents and we stored the memory of these for use in later episodes.

Hugh Paddick and Betty Marsden were just superbly professional and when the audience was in (and the studio in Lower Regent Street was always packed for *Round the Horne*) they gave the most polished West End performances. One great treat that Marty and I allowed ourselves when writing the script was to create strange things for the announcer, Douglas Smith, to say and odd roles for him to play. Our particular delight was that when Douglas got a laugh, which with his laid-back delivery and elegant manner he frequently did, he blushed to the roots of his hair. I don't think the Announcers' common room at Broadcasting House had prepared him for the raucous response of the *Round the Horne* audience, but he stuck to it manfully and was a great asset to the programme.

Of course the comic announcer had long been a tradition in BBC comedy shows, Wallace Greenslade in *The Goon Show* being perhaps the best of them (until Douglas Smith, that is!)

But good as the supporting players were, the star of the show was undoubtedly Kenneth Horne, ex-Cambridge, ex-Wing Commander, ex-business man, a joyous, lovable, amusing, generous friend, companion and father figure to the entire cast and production team.

After each series he'd throw a party, usually a luncheon, and there were presents for everyone. As a group we tried to match his generosity, and with the mutual respect, affection and esteem that *Round the Horne* generated the atmosphere of sixty-six shows which were made was always sunny, and it was, cliché though it may sound, the happiest of programmes. I think that that too comes through and has helped the show to last in the public's affection as long as it has.

Marty departed after we'd written fifty shows to join John Cleese, Graham Chapman, Tim Brooke-Taylor, and 'the lovely Aimi MacDonald' in *At Last the 1948 Show* and for a while, although in constant contact, we didn't write together.

In 1968 I was joined on the writing team by Johnnie Mortimer and Brian Cooke and an actor-writer, Donald Webster, although after a few programmes he dropped out. Mortimer and Cooke, almost at the start of their highly successful tv career, wrote some excellent stuff, mainly sketches, while I concentrated on Julian and Sandy and Rambling Syd Rumpo.

Mortimer and Cooke did create one character that sticks in the mind, a neurotic Australian constantly suspicious of English men's intentions, called Judy Coolibah:

KENNETH: And now in the studio, all the way from the shark-infested beaches of South Kensington, Miss Judy Coolibah.

BETTY: (*Australian*) Too right, sport. Keep yer distance, I've got me police whistle ready.

KENNETH: No need for that, I assure you.

BETTY: That's what you say. How do I know you haven't fixed this chair I'm sitting in, eh? One touch of some hidden button an' steel clamps could spring and fasten every limb ... an' then you'd pounce!

KENNETH: I never even *thought* of such a thing.

BETTY: That's what's wrong with you poms ... no imagination.

KENNETH: Yes, well, shall we carry on? I'll rephrase that, shall we continue? What are you working on now?

BETTY: I'm workin' in a menswear shop. It's disgustin'! One feller came up to me ... 'Yes?' I said ... an' that set 'im goin'. 'You got any ties?' he said, gettin' all personal. Well, I let him have it!

KENNETH: Really? You surprise me.

BETTY: Right across the chops with me genuine Abo boomerang. Another Pom comes in ... 'Can I try on a pair of trousers in the window?' he says. Well, I wasn't havin' *that*! I gave him a quick karate chop in the throat. (*Slightly perplexed*) Didn't get any more customers in that day.

KENNETH: Things were slack?

BETTY: What d'you mean by that?

KENNETH: Nothing, nothing.

BETTY: An' then, you'll hardly believe this, I found a bit o' cardboard attached to a sweater with obscene printin' on it. 'Large Gent's', it said, an' we all know what *that* means.

KENNETH: That was just the ticket.

BETTY: It may be just the ticket to you, but I think it's disgustin'.

KENNETH: Thank you, Judy Coolibah ... And whatever you do, don't let them get you down ... always assuming they wanted to.

The show remained as popular with the public but financial restraints and cutbacks meant that Eddie Braden and the

Hornblowers, a big band, were replaced by an equally musicianly but smaller group under the direction of Max Harris, and The Fraser Hayes Four and Bill Pertwee got the chop. For me somehow the atmosphere had gone as without Marty the stimulus of writing the show was no longer there.

Another series was planned for 1969 but before that could take place Kenneth Horne died.

He died in dramatic circumstances on the stage at the Dorchester Hotel during the 1969 BAFTA Awards presentation. The occasion was hosted by Earl Mountbatten, and Kenneth and Marty and I had just been up to collect our BAFTA award for the 'Best Light Entertainment Script' for the television show *Marty*. Kenneth collapsed, fell from the podium and although mouth-to-mouth resuscitation was tried and Kenneth was rushed by ambulance to St George's Hospital at Hyde Park Corner, he was dead on arrival.

It was the end of a splendid career and for me virtually the end of radio scriptwriting, for although I was now involved in panel games, quizzes, etc., and was to continue to be so for the next twenty years, I wrote very little for the medium.

The BBC in the person of Con Mahoney, who was by now in the Head of Light Entertainment's chair, told me I was unprofessional when I said I hadn't the heart to continue with the show scheduled to replace *Round the Horne*, but when Kenneth died a part of me died too and I mourn him still.

The replacement *Stop Messing About* starring Kenneth Williams, Joan Sims and Hugh Paddick was not a great success and was soon dropped.

Marty Feldman and I were coming to the end of our working partnership too and by 1969 our ten hectic years writing together drew peacefully and in the friendliest manner to a close.

We remained friends to the end of his life but never again sat side by side at our desk shrieking with laughter at some appalling idea with which to irritate or stimulate our audiences.

The story of my writing with Marty is not over. We had done a lot of tv and a movie together. Marty had become a star and before the final curtain there was still an act of mixed farce and drama to unfold with the television series *Marty*.

10

Marty the TV Series

The tv series *Marty* was a ragbag of sketches plus some musical items with a cast of excellent comedy actors including Tim Brooke-Taylor, John Junkin and Roland McLeod. Although Marty and I wrote most of it there were occasional contributions from John Cleese and Graham Chapman, Michael Palin and Terry Jones, John Junkin, Donald Webster and the American animator Terry Gilliam. Our main themes were soccer, time and human beings who were misfits.

Soccer was the middle-class obsession in the late sixties, an obsession inspired mainly by Brian Glanville, the writer of elegant prose on the subject, and hordes of intellectuals of all shades of radical thought could be seen most Sunday mornings hacking each other's ankles in Hyde Park.

In *Marty* we tackled the subject of soccer (no pun intended) with a profile of an imaginary footballer, Danny Gruntfuttock, and a sketch where a referee taking a player's name for fouling an opponent realises that the player is his long-lost illegitimate son. In another sketch we lampooned the xenophobic BBC soccer commentators, and in yet another Marty as a randy South American centre-forward propositions the lady VIP who is shaking hands with the players before the match and chases her lustfully down the field, grounding her finally in the goalmouth.

Apart from playing occasionally for a 'show biz' eleven in which Leonard Rossiter was the star player and from which I retired after being kicked on the knee by a jockey, or rather a failed jockey, a brute of a stable boy who'd outgrown his vocation and vented his frustration on me, Marty and I would go to football matches to unwind after a week's hard writing. There, like the psychiatrist who goes to a strip show and watches the audience, we listened keenly to the aficionados at Chelsea, Fulham or the Arsenal whose comments on the game were not infrequently more entertaining than the games themselves. We treasured the cries of 'You've only got the pigeons to beat' when in an unlikely breakaway a Fulham winger would race for the opponent's goal, or over a disputed offside decision, 'The judge had the flute in his mouth ten minutes before he shot' (meaning of course that the referee had blown his whistle, fractionally before the goal was scored, for some unspecified offence).

In those days anyone could go to a match without fear of abuse or attack and Lyn, who has been a lifelong Fulham supporter, would, when in her teens, travel from Lingfield where she lived to Craven Cottage, stand in the boys' enclosure and return home completely unperturbed. Who would let their teenage daughter do such a thing today? We gave up going twenty years ago, and while I know and respect many fine soccer players I'd need a lot of persuasion to go near any First Division football ground on match day.

Back in 1969, though, things were different and soccer provided us with useful material with which to get laughs.

Time seems an unlikely theme for comedy, but it occurred to me that while it only takes a fraction of a second to think of something – eating a superb meal, for instance, or playing a great round of golf – these things all take time and preparation.

Marty agreed that it was an interesting idea to pursue, and our first venture into this dichotomy of aspiration and achievement was called 'The Three Minute Coach Trip'. In the late sixties the inexpensive coach tour of Europe was popular and firms would advertise 'Five Countries in Three Days'. We boiled this down to an outing to the seaside that took, on screen, exactly three minutes. The location shooting took some days, but with a taut script, speeded-up film and expert cutting the result was very satisfactory. Marty in bowler hat and dirty raincoat lagging behind a group of middle-aged day trippers, with an anguished cry of 'Wait for me!', was splendidly funny.

Our next sketch along those lines was more ambitious. We

called it 'The Night Life of a Chartered Accountant' and it was one of our few sketches with a sex theme. The setting is the bedroom of a lower middle-class household in suburbia.

Husband (Marty) and wife (Anne Lancaster) are in bed. She is nagging him about some trivial domestic matter.

As she speaks he mumbles, 'I forgot to put the cat out', and in his pyjamas leaves the room.

Cut to: Exterior of house. Night. Marty emerges, now in full evening dress plus opera cape and top hat, leaps into his Morris Minor and speeds away.

Next shot: The car draws up outside an elegant apartment block. Marty gets out of car and enters the building.

Cut to: Interior. Elegant bedroom. A beautiful young woman, in the traditional flimsy negligee, embraces Marty as he enters. They drink champagne. He throws her on the bed.

Cut to: The Morris Minor arriving back at suburban house. Marty gets out of car and enters house.

Cut to: Bedroom – as before.

The wife is completing the sentence she started as her husband originally left the room.

So far so good, but taking our writing lives in our hands we developed the theme still further with two other exploits, each wilder than the one before.

Eventually the husband staggers back into the matrimonial bedroom, pulls the bedclothes over himself and settles down to sleep. The wife smiles winningly and in a voice of unambiguous sexuality croons: 'Darling.' The husband snores. The wife, rebuffed by this, complains bitterly: 'That's the trouble with you these days. You're always too tired.' End of sketch, which ran for about six minutes.

I found 'The Night Life of a Chartered Accountant' interesting and satisfying to write, for several reasons. First it explored the idea of sexual fantasy and stretched the fantasy almost to breaking point. It dealt with the whole concept of the speed of thought as against the reality of action in a comprehensible way, and finally one could see not only a frustrating marriage but the reasons for the frustration; he too tired or disinclined to have sex, she, as a result, resentful and nagging.

Two other sketches from that series stand out in my mind.

The first was a scene in a vet's waiting room where Marty takes a pet creature suffering from 'beak and hoof'. The 'creature' was in a theatrical skip, and never seen by the audience, but made a variety of shrieks, moos, grunts and howls. 'What is it?' asks a nervous onlooker. 'I'm not sure,' replies Marty. 'I looked him up in the *British Book of Birds*. He wasn't in that and he wasn't in the *Cattle Breeders Guide*. Eventually I found him in the *Book of Revelations*.'

The sketch, quite funny as it stood, was made much funnier because the creature was unseen. Our old friend the imagination of the audience was brought in to play.

The other sketch was an extension of logic. In golf you play the ball where it lies and it occurred to me that if the ball landed on, say, a lorry load of sand and the lorry drove off the ball should be played from wherever the lorry came to rest.

Taking that as the basis of the sketch we wrote a series of incidents following the persistent golfer and his patient caddy across country via a wedding, a funeral, a railway tunnel, the bathroom of a suburban semi and various other locations until the golfer arrives back on the course. The ball drops two feet from the hole – and the golfer misses his putt, and his second and third. Night falls with the golfer still desperately trying to hole the putt.

Subsequently we wrote other sketches with a similar mixture of reality and fantasy including one which started in a florist's and finished on the Bridge Over the River Kwai, and another where the cast played the puppets in a Punch and Judy show.

*

Marty won the Writers Guild of Great Britain Award for Best Light Entertainment Show, and the BAFTA Award for best script. Marty picked up a host of other awards personally, and at Montreux when it looked a certainty that the programme would get the Gold we were pipped at the post by an excellent Czech entry and were runners-up with the Silver Rose, plus an honourable mention from the Press Jury.

After the second series of *Marty*, which included an amusing conceit about a Speak-Your-Weight machine that falls in love with a commuter, and a sketch in which Marty, as a cockney ballet dancer (in the ballet by courtesy of the Prisoners' Aid Society) is trying to explain to the company manager, played with an air of puzzled despair by John Junkin, why things had gone wrong with the previous night's performance of *The Sleeping Beauty*. The sketch contained lines like: 'Look, Foulwater – er, Ludmenkov – you awaken Sleeping Beauty with a kiss. You do not climb into bed with her, nor do you put your teeth in a glass on the bedside table.' And when it transpires a fight had broken out, 'And where did the spanner come from?' 'I had it in my tights.' 'Oh, well, that answers another question I was going to ask you.' Unsurprisingly it raised a lot of laughter. *Marty* was such a success that Marty Feldman was signed to star in a film we'd written called *Every Home Should Have One*, but we never wrote together again.

At our best I think we were the equal of any British comedy writers of that time and I feel that if Marty had been content to remain a part of a script-writing team we would have become even more successful and prosperous and that he would still be alive today.

Marty's story has a sad ending. After a patchy but award-winning series for ATV called *The Marty Feldman Comedy Machine* he went to Hollywood and made two pictures with Mel Brooks, *Young Frankenstein* and *Silent Movie*. Brooks's verdict on Marty is that 'he could be heaven or hell', always wanting to do another take and never content with what he had done but on his day sublimely gifted. Marty could be like that when we were writing together, never wanting to finish a script and spending hours searching for a better ending. My attitude was blunt: 'From here on anything we write is for the wastepaper basket. They just aren't buying half-hour scripts that run for forty minutes this year.'

After Mel Brooks, Marty made a film with Gene Wilder, *Sherlock Holmes's Smarter Brother* which was mildly successful, and two films which Marty co-wrote and directed. One, *The Last Remake of Beau Geste*, was bad, and *In God We Trust* was a disaster.

Marty died of a heart attack alone in Mexico City during the shooting of *Yellowbeard the Pirate*, a self-indulgent flop made by a group formed around Graham Chapman in which Marty, as an act of friendship, had been given a small part.

Towards the end of his life he drank heavily and was certainly into soft drugs and, I would guess, some of the slightly less soft ones as well.

I loved him as a brother but, as brothers can, he exasperated me too. Emotionally he was either up or down. Through the many years we knew each other there were times when I know I irritated him profoundly, but there were also times when his ego led him into acts of childish anger, misjudgment or conceit which would have been laughable if they hadn't been so counterproductive. Let me give you some examples.

In 1965 we were asked to write for a brand new comedian who was to be the new compère of the revived *Sunday Night at the London Palladium*. His name was Jimmy Tarbuck and he was appearing in summer season at Great Yarmouth. Marty and I went to see the show, liked what we saw of this bright, brash, cheery newcomer and agreed to write for him.

After two weeks however we realised that Jimmy Tarbuck though funny with the gags he knew was scared of anything completely new and, as any comic would, reverted to tried and trusted material – 'I said to the waiter "Have you got frog's legs?" He said "Yes". I said "Well, hop over the counter and get us some" ' – was a typical example, and though the audience loved it the critics didn't. Milton Shulman wrote a devastating article about Tarbuck and his Palladium debut and, as our names were on the screen as scriptwriters, blamed us for the far from golden oldies that Tarbuck was using to wow the customers.

On reading Milton Shulman's piece, Marty immediately became temperamental and refused to write for Tarbuck any more. He also threw a tantrum because of a supposed slight by Kenneth More who was a guest on one of the shows. We got out of the contract, but rather unfairly I got the blame.

I didn't meet Jimmy Tarbuck until twenty years after, when I explained what had happened and the air was cleared at last.

Much later when Marty was a rising Hollywood star he was asked to make a presentation at the Academy Awards ceremony. The writer allocated to work with him was the charming and experienced Hal Kanter. Kanter suggested one comedy routine involving the coat sleeves of Marty's dinner jacket getting longer and longer, which could have been very funny as a piece of silent comedy.

Marty's strength had never been his vocal dexterity. At our wedding reception (in 1965) Marty, who was my best man and who had a very warm brother/sister relationship with Lyn, proposed the toast to the 'happy couple'. He made something of a hash of it and became tongue-tied, at which Frankie Howerd, who was one of our guests, said loudly, 'Thank God he can write!'

However, back at the Oscars, Marty didn't care for the sleeve business and, without consulting Kanter, decided on another gag. He had made for him a plaster replica of an Oscar which, as he was presenting it, he would drop and it would shatter. Not a great gag, but it had an authentic touch of the Marty Feldman mayhem and could have gone quite well. Unfortunately when he dropped the bogus Oscar it *didn't* shatter, and to make matters worse Marty then jumped up and down on it, breaking the plaster replica into small pieces. To the cream of Hollywood assembled for the ceremony who weren't in on the gag it looked like a piece of wanton vandalism, and jumping on an Oscar was sacrilege. That night Marty lost a lot of friends.

During the making of *Every Home Should Have One* Marty developed 'a touch of the grandeurs' – a chauffeur-driven Rolls Royce on call twenty-four hours a day and every conceivable luxury had wafted him into an unreal world.

Now he and I had been working on this screenplay together for over two years. The original story, about an advertising man approaching the male menopause who decides to employ an au pair and as a result has various sexual fantasies, was invented by Herbert Kretzmer and Milton Shulman, and Ned Sherrin was the producer. Marty and I wrote and re-wrote several versions of the screenplay, latterly with Richard Chamberlain in mind (well, he was in somebody's mind at Columbia Pictures, whose project *Every Home* was).

As time went on it seemed less and less likely that the film would be made, but then Marty became a television star in Britain. I convinced Ned Sherrin that Marty should play the lead, but because Marty wasn't box office in the States Columbia weren't keen. Sherrin did a deal whereby he bought the movie from Columbia and sold it to British Lion and we went into production.

The film was directed by Jim Clark, who was (and is) a great film editor but who had little experience of directing. Marty had always worked better with a stronger personality – John Cleese, Tim Brooke-Taylor and I had at one time or another operated in that capacity, as had Dennis Main Wilson, who directed the *Marty* tv series.

Jim Clark, though charming and thoroughly professional, was not tough. No Otto Preminger he, and Marty deferred to on every hand became swollen-headed. I didn't see much of the filming as I was involved in other work, but when I did visit the studio at Shepperton, Marty's attitude was condescending.

We had constructed a very elaborate chase sequence to end the film, which on paper certainly worked and I felt, as Marty did when we wrote it, that it was fast, funny and original. But Marty in his new role as Master of the Universe decided the film needed a new, different and better ending. I suggested bringing in Michael Palin and Terry Jones with whom I was currently working at Thames Television, but Marty said he wanted Denis Norden.

So Denis Norden was brought in and wrote a new ending to the film which was neither funny nor filmable. Marty and Jim Clark then decided that they'd ad lib the ending. Marty had little experience of films and Jim had little experience of comedy and between them they managed to make a mess of it.

There was a lot more wrong with the film too and it wasn't much of a success at the box office.

Years later Marty apologised to me for the way he'd behaved. 'I don't know what came over me,' he said. I didn't have the heart to tell him.

11

Monty Python and Hollywood Hills

I have to back-track a little here because 1968–69 were hectic years.

At one time or another during those two years I was writing *Round the Horne* with Johnnie Mortimer and Brian Cooke, script-editing a tv series also starring Kenneth Horne for ABC tv called *Horne A'Plenty*, script-editing a tv series for Tommy Cooper, also for ABC, and chairing the radio panel game *Sounds Familiar*.

I came to chair *Sounds Familiar* in a roundabout way.

In 1968 the old BBC radio stations, Home, Light and Third Programme were to be replaced by Radios 1, 2, 3 and 4, but there was an awkward gap of ten weeks that had to be filled in the Light Entertainment schedule. It was decided to make a pilot programme of a show business quiz, called *I Remember Lola Tickle*, devised by Denis Gifford and produced by my *Round the Horne* colleague John Simmonds. John was worried about it and asked me to come to the recording of the pilot programme and give him my reactions. I duly turned up and watched. My first reaction was that it was far too complicated. There were two teams of four panellists, one lot armed with buzzers and the other with bells. There was a chairman, Jimmy Hanley, and a mystery guest – who turned out to be Arthur Askey. Now, to cram all that into thirty minutes seemed an impossibility. My suggestion was to reduce the two panels to one of four people, lose the buzzers and bells and make the show more one of reminiscence and less of competition, and ask Arthur Askey to be the chairman. As an afterthought I suggested that the title be changed. (Lola Tickle, by the way, was a character in *ITMA*, played many years before by Maurice Denham.)

John Simmonds's secretary. Susan Barnes, came up with *Sounds Familiar* for the title, and John Simmonds, as a thank-you for my help, asked me to chair the ten programmes scheduled.

The ten programmes became well over a hundred, as *Sounds Familiar* became quite a success with panellists such as Tommy Trinder, Arthur Marshall, Wilfrid Pickles, 'Monsewer' Eddie Gray, Dame Anna Neagle, Jack Warner, Ernie Wise (at the time when Eric Morecambe's first heart attack had put him out of action), Ray Alan and Lord Charles, Albert Modley, Alfie Bass, Sheila Hancock, George Melly, Douglas Byng and many more, delivering original and amusing anecdotes.

It ran until 1974 when Denis Gifford, having fallen out with the BBC, took the idea to Thames Television, where it re-emerged as *Looks Familiar*, hosted by Denis Norden.

My favourite moment of *Sounds Familiar* was when Michael Wilding was a guest. At first he was shy and diffident, but he soon warmed up and brought the house down with an anecdote about Noël Coward in a restaurant, sending back the woodcock he'd ordered with the clipped comment, 'Too much wood – not enough cock.'

Meanwhile I was working with Marty Feldman on *Marty*, producing a second series of *Horne A'Plenty* for the newly created Thames Television, acting as Comedy Consultant to Thames and adapting *The World of Beachcomber*, from the *Daily Express* column written by J.B. Morton, for the BBC.

At the end of 1968 my consultancy at Thames came to an end – my relationship with the company had always been somewhat uneasy, and though as a script editor I'd worked well, as a producer I was not a success. Through the latter series of *Horne A'Plenty* Kenneth Horne was clearly a sick man, and after his death in '69 I was, for the time being, without anything of real interest to do.

Then I was approached by Tom Sloan with an offer to become adviser to BBC tv's Comedy Department. The deal was that they would pay me what Tom Sloan described as a peppercorn rent, that's to say a salary of £3000 per annum, but the implication was that I could write as much as I wanted at my regular fee and, to quote the Eric Idle sketch from *Monty Python's Flying Circus*, 'Nudge nudge, wink wink, say no more!'

My boss was a dynamic lunatic by the name of Michael Mills, who was the Head of Comedy. The Head of Variety was Bill Cotton Jnr. The commitment of the two departments was four hundred shows per annum from the Variety Department, and two hundred shows per annum from the Comedy Department. Tom Sloan oversaw it all. When I arrived there wasn't a lot going on in the Comedy Department apart from a series starring Tessie O'Shea.

We needed new shows badly and Mills and I soon came to the understanding that although we might argue fiercely over what we wanted and how we could achieve it, once agreed there would be no further arguments. The system worked well as I liked and admired Michael Mills for his energy and courage and, apart from occasional lapses, his taste. He had been the original producer of *The Walrus and the Carpenter* and a stabilising factor in the mayhem that surrounded the second *Marty* series when it was discovered that the producer, Dennis Main Wilson, had spent the entire budget for the series on the pre-series filming.

That was sorted out to nobody's entire satisfaction, but the success of the series soon allowed everyone to forget the earlier contretemps.

Roger Race earns a mention for his role in these proceedings, for at the beginning of *Marty* he was the Floor Manager but by the end he'd become an excellent director and was responsible for many of the cleverer pieces of technical wizardry based on the ideas Marty and I had dreamed up.

But that was now in the past, and Mills and I got down to the business of sorting out what we wanted to see on the screen in the Comedy Department in the future.

*

My first contribution, brought to me by my old friend Ned Sherrin, was a series he wanted to produce written by N.F. Simpson ('Wally', after Mrs Wallace Simpson, to his friends) and called *World in Ferment*. It was a parody of the more serious magazine programmes, and the scripts read well.

The BBC commissioned all concerned, and Ned Sherrin's flair for casting was again evident as those involved included Arthur Lowe, Angela Thorne, Jack Shepherd, Eleanor Bron and the irreplaceable Irene Handl. Week by week she was interviewed about her life as a Woolworth's supervisor; the stories of what to her was a dramatic and exciting career being touched, as always in his writing, by N.F. Simpson's surreal brilliance. From memory I quote:

INTERVIEWER: I believe King George V and Queen Mary visited your store on one occasion.

SUPERVISOR: Oh, yes. They were shown round and when they came to me, Queen Mary said to the King, 'We've seen this one before.' We had arranged for them to purchase something and saw to it that they were short-changed. They were very amused by that.

The director of *World in Ferment* was Roger Ordish, who with David O'Clee had joined BBC Radio from Trinity College, Dublin, and both transferred to television as directors. They were clever, interesting men, both with a laid-back sense of humour.

Once *World in Ferment* was launched I turned my attention to two other projects. One was to get Barry Humphries onto the tv screen in Britain. His one-man show at the Fortune Theatre in 1969 had caused a certain amount of interest and he had, of course, done television work in Australia.

At first the BBC were dubious, as one or two of the hierarchy were not too keen on 'female impersonation', as Barry's depiction of Edna Everage was regarded. Some of his other characters, such as Sandy Stone, were thought to be too parochial for a large audience to enjoy, and his Sir Les Patterson had yet to be born; but by doing a bit of desk-pounding I got my way and a Barry Humphries special was made, directed by David O'Clee and produced by Dennis Main Wilson.

In those days, although at first we didn't know it, Barry Humphries had a serious drink problem. He was, in fact, an alcoholic and only gave up when some years later he was told that if he kept on drinking in the way he did he only had six weeks to live.

The way he drank in '69 you'd put his life expectancy at six hours, and Dennis Main Wilson, an intense, gnarled whippet of a man was also a heavy drinker. The Humphries special was a great success and he was given a series, but the booze got to him and the series was a flop. It was a terrible waste of time; for sober, as he is permanently today, Barry Humphries is one of the most brilliant, gifted entertainers in the world. Drunk he's something else again, and it's a mercy that, unlike Tony Hancock, Sid Field and Marty Feldman among others, he was able to give up the demon drink before it was too late.

*

My other project in mid '69 was altogether more complicated.

Through working with so many writers and performers I had unconsciously been putting together in my mind the bones of a new revue-type show – a follow-on from *Marty*. The people I wanted for it were John Cleese and Graham Chapman from *The Frost Report* and *At Last the 1948 Show* and Michael Palin and Terry Jones from the Thames TV children's programme *Do Not Adjust Your Set*. I sounded them out about working together and they said they were more or less agreeable, but Palin and Jones asked if Eric Idle and Terry Gilliam could be included in the team.

All six had worked together, or at least knew each other, and it seemed to me that the interaction, one upon the other, of these intelligent and gifted men would produce something of lasting value. We had one or two meetings and I went to Michael Mills with the proposition. Mills said of me at that time, 'Barry Took asks you a question but half way through you realise he's giving you an order.'

When it came to my six he was dubious, and Tom Sloan was even more worried – mainly by what he foresaw as an extremely expensive show. I persisted. Michael Mills complained that I was behaving as arrogantly as Baron von Richtofen, the World War One air ace whose squadron was known in the RAF as Baron von Richtofen's Flying Circus. I became known as Baron von Took, and Cleese, Palin and Co. as *my* flying circus. All the memos relating to the proposed programme referred to it as 'The Circus' and when at last we received the agreement to go ahead no title for the show had been decided.

During my battle with the BBC I also had battles with the cast. We'd have a meeting in my flat, agreements about style and format would be reached and the team would depart for home. Within an hour the first worried member of The Circus would call asking if going into a team show would interrupt or even destroy their career. At one time or another they all touched on this theme and my reply was always the same. 'If it's a hit it can't possibly hurt your career. If it's a flop it'll be over and forgotten very soon.' Then the BBC came up with another problem. How were we going to pay them? My answer was 'Decide the amount you wish to spend on the cast, divide by six and pay each of the cast one sixth of the total. Do the same with the script fee and your problem is solved.' 'But someone might write more than someone else.' I said, 'That's their problem.'

My final comment was 'We've got six gifted and intelligent people, let's trust them.' And trust them we did. The title of the first script they submitted was 'Owl Stretching Time', the second they called 'Whither Canada?' Michael Mills was adamant that these titles were not what he wanted. In fact he issued an edict that as the show was known in all the BBC internal correspondence as 'The Flying Circus', those words must appear in the title.

I believe it was John Cleese who actually added the 'Monty Python', but *Monty Python's Flying Circus* it became, and I think it would be fair to say it didn't hurt anybody's career.

The funny thing is that I never suspected that it would be that popular or successful. My belief was that it would attract a minority, possibly a cult, audience but, more important, that it would influence the thinking about other sketch shows and generate new ideas. In fact it had no effect on any other show at all but became a worldwide best seller, first on television and then on record, on stage, in books and in films.

It became a cult all right – possibly the largest cult ever in show business. At first it received only scant attention, but as the word went round that *Python* was something special it soon became a much sought-after programme.

The Pythons suspected censorship but I can only remember two occasions when there was any comment. The first, after an early recording, was Tom Sloan asking, 'Does John Cleese have to say bastard twice?'

The other was much later, when there was a wine-tasting sketch in which the subject, or even possibly the act, of drinking urine was promoted. 'What can we do?' I was asked. My answer was simple, let them record it and then cut it. I think it was Terry Jones who was always trying to roll back the frontiers of taste, Gilliam seemed happy inventing crazy animations, Graham Chapman (who, sadly, died in 1989 aged 48) gave some splendid performances, Eric Idle was something of a loner and stern critic of the group, and the stars were undoubtedly John Cleese and Michael Palin whose work together was quite wonderful. The Cheese Shop, the Dead Parrot, the Argument Centre, and the Ministry of Funny Walks sketches became classics.

The two BBC men who saw *Python* through its early struggles were directors Ian McNaughton and John Howard Davies.

The only real woman in the cast was Carol Cleveland, and the rest of the female parts were taken by the Pythons themselves, but whether they did this for sake of economy or because they enjoyed dressing up I never discovered.

In Los Angeles recently I was delighted to see, on some obscure television channel, some early *Python* programmes shown without commercial breaks, and just as fresh as they were over twenty years ago.

*

With *Python* established on BBC 1 and Barry Humphries set for production on BBC 2, I was free to accept an offer from producer George Schlatter to join the writing team of *Rowan and Martin's Laugh In* in Hollywood. The BBC froze my contract – that is to say, they gave me three months' unpaid leave, and after some delay by the US Immigration Department over work permits (much better and more efficient today, incidentally) Lyn and I with Elinor, then sixteen months old, took the TWA flight from London to Los Angeles.

On arrival, after an eleven-hour flight during which Elinor stayed awake and cheerful for the entire journey, we duly staggered into LA Immigration to find that the permit issued in London wasn't a work permit at all but merely a visitor's permit. The official gave me a broad wink and said, 'If you tell me you're here for a vacation I'll believe you.' So I told him just that, and we were in the USA for the first time.

The visa was duly amended and I now have a permanent right to work in the USA. I'm also a member of the Writers' Guild of America (West) and have good relations with many American script writers, but back in '69 I knew no one – and, it goes without saying, no one knew me.

Marty Feldman was as yet unknown on the Hollywood scene, and Britain, while revered for its fine dramatic actors, had only rarely broken through in the USA in comedy. Admittedly two of the cinema's greatest funny men, Charlie Chaplin and Stan Laurel, were English, but although Bob Hope originally came from England he couldn't by any stretch of the imagination be regarded as an English funny man, his humour being absolutely American both in style and delivery. Benny Hill had yet to make his impact. As for English writers, apart from Bernard Shaw and Oscar Wilde who were of course Irish, they were to all intents and purposes unknown.

George Schlatter, however, liked to employ Brits. I think he felt lucky with them. One of his principal advisers at the conception of *Laugh In* was Digby Wolfe (whom I had worked with years before on an American game show imported to Britain called *Laughline*), and Judy Carne was a big hit from the start of *Laugh In*. Roddy Maude-Roxby appeared in the early episodes but wasn't terribly happy or terribly effective in the show.

For the series in which I was to have my brief association with the show, the tall, couth actor/writer Jeremy Lloyd had become a regular member of the team. When I arrived in November half the series had been written and there were two new writers added to the group which totalled, on average, fifteen people. Allan Manings was the head writer, and Marc London and David Panich were called the writing supervisors.

London and Panich were the original odd couple. David was a

fey, disturbed genius who had several spells in mental homes, was a drug addict and was given to moments of wild eccentricity that counterbalanced his normally calm, quiet exterior. The only native-born Californian of the group, he was a tragic figure but a genuine original.

Marc London (both names assumed) was more like a screen gangster than a comedy script writer. He was as tough-minded as Panich was woolly, and very businesslike. To him scripts were products and the artistic merit depended on audience reaction (which as it was 'canned', i.e. put on after recording, wasn't an infallible guide).

During my time with *Laugh In* his application to change his name by deed poll came through. His name had been one of those mittel-European names full of z's and w's and with few vowels – let's say Zrabrvorwckzy. I remarked, on hearing that Marc was now officially called London, that as an act of reciprocal appreciation the capital of England had changed its name to Zrabrvorwckzy. A small enough joke, but *Rowan and Martin's Laugh In* was a vast assembly of small jokes, developed with machine-gun rapidity by probably the best cast of any American tv show ever mounted.

Dan Rowan and Dick Martin were an interesting study in contrasts. Dick Martin was a toothy, goofy actor who'd appeared with Lucille Ball in one of her hit series and whose main interest in life was golf. Dan Rowan was intense, a committed liberal, full of frustration about the corruption in Washington, the war in Vietnam and the direction in which the USA was heading.

The Right and Left lined up pretty well 50/50 through both the writing and the performing teams with the usual percentage of 'don't knows' in the middle.

I was faintly amused by it all. Although for my $1000 a programme I wasn't getting much on the screen and was finding it extremely difficult to adapt to the American production-line technique – '15 Writers No Waiting' – I did learn a great deal from the people I met on the show.

Let me give you the geographical set-up, which was important to the various relationships between management and writers and performers, and NBC who screened the series.

Anyone who remembers *Rowan and Martin's Laugh In* will

recall that it was set in 'Beautiful Downtown Burbank'. Now, Burbank is not that beautiful and it is, to all intents and purpose, *all* downtown; a mish-mash of film and television studios, factories, restaurants, motels and apartment blocks. The smog that casts an almost permanent pall over greater Los Angeles settles too on Burbank, which is in effect a northern suburb of the city. George Schlatter and Ed Friendly's offices were spacious, air-conditioned and well-furnished but strictly functional. The contract President Nixon signed when he appeared on the show, suitably framed, was just one of the pieces of memorabilia that adorned the walls.

Here George Schlatter and his co-producer Ed Friendly, a quiet man who looked after the marketing side of the show, had their separate offices. Here too Allan Manings, London and Panich, and Coslough Johnson and Jeremy Lloyd had their offices, and secretaries and various assistants filled whatever space was left over.

The rest of the writing team worked two to a suite in a motel opposite Warner Brothers Studios, some four hundred yards away. It sounds more opulent than it was, for in appearance the motel was somewhat dilapidated and the suites consisting of bedroom, living room/kitchen, bathroom and so on were by no means five-star.

As far as I could see when I arrived, writers were put together to work in pairs quite arbitrarily. For a while I worked with Jim Abell (who seemed to spend most of his time writing scripts for other shows). Then I was teamed with Jim Mulligan, a shortish neurotic from Maryland who would hit the typewriter when it failed to deliver a joke. I think he felt insecure as his wife was a much more romantic person and he was deeply pragmatic. Their house overlooked the ocean and from their windows they could watch schools of whales making their way south to mate. This didn't seem to move Jim Mulligan too much and he was uptight with one tension or another most of the time. His comment to his wife, when later they visited us in London, was: 'Hey, they've got the john in a room of its own.' Clearly a novelty to him to see the lavatory and bathroom separated. His wife, on the other hand, found England a fairyland, a place she'd always dreamed of and on seeing it for real finding her dream had come true.

Jim Mulligan is, alas, dead, felled by a heart attack. I hope Mrs Mulligan is continuing to find life a romantic adventure.

My next writing partner was the excellent Gene Farmer who came originally from a small town near the Canadian border, called Birmidgee, and with whom for some weeks I wrote 'The Fickle Finger of Fate', an item which pointed out corruption in government or mismanagement in industry. Gene looked and spoke like someone from a small mid-western town, was tight with a dime, but was an original and inventive writer, and a very good companion.

His one oddity was that he would only eat in the local restaurant on Thursday when clam chowder was on the menu. That he or any of the writing team should eat lunch at a restaurant was unthought of until I arrived on the scene.

George Schlatter, in addition to providing rooms where his writers could work, also provided them with the necessities of life and I was astounded on my first Monday when a man appeared to take orders. The writers would ask for diet Pepsi, cheese, crackers, cookies, milk, coffee, tea bags, toilet paper, writing paper, typewriter ribbons and any other commodity they felt they needed. Some would over-order and take the unused portions of the week's rations home. To me from England, where scriptwriting was (and still is) as Denis Norden described it 'a cottage industry', this was weird. Burbank was more like Fritz Lang's Metropolis than a Scottish weaver's hovel. As the set-up was explained to me, 'George doesn't like us taking lunch.' I said – in my best stiff-upper-lip manner, 'I haven't come eight thousand miles not to have lunch', and at one o'clock I set off across the road to the nearby Hyatt House restaurant, accompanied by one brave soul who defied the 'no lunch' order.

The next day another writer joined us and within a week all ten of us at the motel were taking a midday break. The jokes that were made during those lunch hours were infinitely better than many that were written for the show.

Christmas in Los Angeles lasts one day and by Boxing Day everything is back to normal. The *Laugh In* team had a short break and then it was back to the grindstone for the remainder of the series. One week Jack Benny was the guest and we all duly turned in jokes about Jack being stingy and vain and when the script was assembled (about the size and shape of a London telephone directory) George went through it with assistant producer Caroline Raskin and *hated* it.

Normally writing for *Laugh In* was a strictly nine-to-five job and the covers went on the typewriter at precisely 5 pm whether the joke was finished or not, but on this occasion a small group of us assembled in George Schlatter's office after hours and listened while he tore the script to pieces and asked for new ideas.

George was eventually satisfied that we'd solved the problem at around 2.30 am. In the meantime food and drink had been brought to us (coffee and cheeseburgers) and I arrived back at our temporary Hollywood home with the worst attack of indigestion ever, plus a splitting headache and a strong desire to get on the next plane to England.

Shortly after I'd joined the team the performing part of the company was augmented by Lily Tomlin, brought in to replace Judy Carne. She was terrific, an immediate success, and in her role as Ermintrude, the telephonist calling Gore Vidal ('Hello, Mr Veedle?') and other notables ('Hello, Milhouse') brought a new dimension to the series.

All in all, working in that set-up was stimulating and exciting and I think that I helped if not with too many jokes then at least to shift attitudes around a little. For example, writers rarely went to recordings, which went on all day and into the evenings. The shows were not recorded in front of an invited audience but parties of tourists would be led into the audience seating area, allowed to watch the stop-start recording of the show for a few minutes and then shepherded out by NBC ushers.

In the evening friends and relatives could, if they wanted, go into the studio and watch, and one evening I took Lyn along. In a break in recording we went down onto the studio floor to talk to the actors. Danny Kaye was the principal guest that week and as he'd recently returned from the UK I wanted to get his reaction to his visit.

Anyway, Lyn looked stunning in a grey outfit with pink trimmings: very smart, very European and extremely chic. In seconds she was surrounded by the male members of the group and George Schlatter was charm itself.

This sort of thing would be commonplace in British television, but in the States such was separation of the roles of production, performance and writing it seemed extremely novel that a writer and his wife should venture onto the studio floor and talk as equals to the cast and the producer.

Incidentally, Danny Kaye had been interviewed by Simon Dee, then a popular chat show host (and more of him later) in the back of a London taxi as it drove up Park Lane, and Kaye wondered how it had come out. I was able to tell him that the filmed interview had been a great success and he was delighted at the news, being an ardent anglophile.

When we'd heard that he was coming on the show, and knowing his penchant for English accents, I was asked if I would write some typically English jokes. I said, 'Do you mean the jokes we laugh at in England or jokes that sound English to you?'

I was told 'I guess we mean the second one', and I remembered an oldie about two Englishmen, a father and son, in a railway compartment travelling through East Anglia. An American joins them and goes into eulogies about the great times he'd had in that part of England during the war and particularly the hospitality of the local lady of the manor, who apparently adored American servicemen and had granted her sexual favours to everyone over the rank of Sergeant. 'Gee, she was great. One of the great bedfellows of all time. We called her "the horizontal duchess".' At this point the elderly Englishman, who is deaf, says to his son 'What's he saying?' To which the son replies, 'He says he knows Mother.'

By hamming it up a bit and overdoing the accents my American colleagues, to whom it was a new joke, found it amazingly funny and I was led round the motel and made to retell the joke to each of the other writing teams.

I had at last broken through and their initial suspicion of this stranger in their midst vanished to be replaced by warm friendship. Lyn and I went to parties given by many of the team, sometimes taking Elinor and sometimes using the services of a baby sitter who, it turned out, was the sister of the actress Debra Paget.

During our three months in Hollywood we stayed at the

Chateau Marmont on Sunset Boulevard where we had a two-bedroom apartment with maid service. It had long been traditional for actors and writers on short contracts to stay at the Chateau Marmont, which even today is unique in that sprawling city of Los Angeles in offering a warm and friendly atmosphere, and when the smog clears wonderful views across the city.

*

For Lyn life in Hollywood wasn't wonderful. She didn't care to drive and walking the streets was not a recommended occupation, filled as they seemed to be with junkies, drunks, and religious fanatics. The only safe and pleasant place to take Elinor was the Los Angeles Zoo, but after a while zoos pall and Lyn was secretly dying to get back home to a more tranquil way of life.

The decision for me was slightly more difficult as I'd grown to like what I was doing and had, in fact, gone native. That's to say I'd visited a menswear shop on Sunset Boulevard and kitted myself out with check shirt, flared trousers equipped with a belt with a huge brass buckle (well, it was 1969), a neckerchief, and a pair of rawhide western boots.

When I turned up to work in this outfit, which I thought was very swish and extremely American, Allan Manings's comment was, 'We thought we'd brought over an English gent. What we've got is a fag cowboy.' After that I wore my American togs at weekends only.

For all its production-line atmosphere and tension, working on the writing team of *Rowan and Martin's Laugh In* was stimulating, and until the smog got to my enfeebled lungs (I was a heavy smoker in those days) I felt fit and eager. By the time my contract was coming to its close I felt very much at home with this strange bunch of human beings who made up the *Laugh In* writing team and had become friends with many of them.

My *best* friend and a good friend still, over twenty years later, was the head writer, Allan Manings. He and his actress wife, Whitney, were kindness itself when Lyn, Elinor and I arrived in LA, and he was a fount of wisdom, good sense and understanding. He tolerated me and helped me to learn how things were done in Hollywood.

You can imagine my feelings when, towards the end of my time in Hollywood, in January 1970, the regular writers of the series made me an offer I had to refuse.

One day nine or ten of the writers invited me into a room for a chat. After a moment or two of gossip the spokesman for the group made a proposition. In effect he said that he and the other writers had talked it over and that when the preparation for the next series of *Laugh In* started they would go to George Schlatter and Ed Friendly and say that they wanted me to be Head Writer.

I was amazed, flattered and then, when the implications became apparent, worried by their offer because it meant that I would have to replace the man who had been my best friend and keenest ally during my time with the group. Had I accepted it would have seemed like an act of betrayal. My BBC contract gave me an honourable way out and I said to the writers who had offered me their allegiance that to accept their offer would mean breaking my agreement with the BBC, something I could not do. They accepted this, threw a party for us before we left LA, and in February 1970 we boarded the TWA LA to London flight and went home.

12

London Weekend

On my return to the BBC in February 1970 I found little had changed. In fact as far as one script was concerned nothing had changed at all.

Just before I'd left for the States, Mike Fentiman, then a producer in the BBC's Presentation Department, and Tony Bilbow, one of the regular presenters of *Late Night Line Up*, had given me a script they'd written and which I thought was very promising. I'd told Michael Mills about it and left it on his desk. It was still there four months later, unread and apparently untouched.

That upset me, and I was further upset, not to say mortified, when Tom Sloan said to me, 'Oh, we didn't expect you to come back. We thought that once you were in America you'd stay there.' I said, 'But my BBC contract ...?' Sloan said, 'Oh, we'd have waived that.'

It seemed a somewhat casual attitude towards something I'd taken very seriously. When my agent, Kenneth Ewing, told me that Stella Richman, the Programme Controller of London Weekend Television, had asked if she could see me, I told him that I would very much like to meet her.

London Weekend Television, originally the brainchild of David Frost, had been granted the commercial television franchise along with Thames in the reorganisation of the ITV companies in 1968. The old Associated Rediffusion had been split up and the capital's ITV channel divided between Thames from Monday to Thursday and LWT from Friday to Sunday.

While Thames, which had absorbed the ABC television

company and a large part of Associated Rediffusion, was, to quote a phrase much used in tv recording, 'running and stable', London Weekend had suffered a number of crises which had culminated in the Managing Director, Michael Peacock, getting the sack and his Programme Controller, Cyril Bennett, and half of the Company's department heads resigning in protest.

This had happened while I was out of the country and I wasn't really aware of the deep trouble the company was in when I had my meeting with Stella Richman.

Stella, a first-class drama script editor and producer, was also the owner of that haunt of international showbusiness in Curzon Street, the White Elephant Club. I found her shrewd, brisk and charming. She offered me the job of Head of Light Entertainment in the reshaped hierarchy of LWT, replacing both Frank Muir, who had been Head of Comedy until the upheaval, and Tito Burns, who had looked after Variety (quiz shows, chat shows, and the song-and-dance programmes).

A variety department is not difficult to run and at its most basic takes little more than a few hours a year to make it tick. Most quiz shows originate in the USA and you can buy them off the peg. With chat shows it's a question of pick your host and set the producer to find whoever happens to be plugging anything that week (a novel, a film, a play) and book them for the programme. It's much the same with what used to be called a tv spectacular. If you wanted Shirley Bassey, for instance, you'd phone her agent, make a deal for so many programmes and then leave it to director, designer, choreographer and the rest to do their stuff and make the Shirley Bassey Show glossy and popular. Repeat the process often enough and you have your year's schedule.

Comedy is much more difficult, for whereas a top variety artiste like Bassey, or Frankie Vaughan, or Max Bygraves is a known quantity, a situation comedy is full of unknown elements. Is the script funny? Can the actors understand it and enhance it? Will the public like it when you've made it? There are a number of imponderables. I'd cut my sit-com teeth on *The Army Game* and *Bootsie and Snudge*, and had advised Thames to put on Mortimer and Cooke's creation, *Father Dear Father*; but while anyone can recognise what will be a hit (as when at the

BBC Michael Mills bought *Up Pompeii* – the broadest of farces, starring Frankie Howerd) there is still a great deal of failure possible however honourable the intentions of the would-be sit-com maker.

I found that what I'd inherited when I moved into my office in Stonebridge Park was a large number of disillusioned, puzzled and depressed producers, assistants and secretaries, suspicious finance controllers, and a general atmosphere of uneasiness. Dr Tom Margerison had replaced Michael Peacock and Stella Richman had taken over from Cyril Bennett, a combination that turned out to be a recipe for disaster. They had inherited, in the heads of department who hadn't resigned when Peacock left, a group of 'barons' who ran their own departments as private concerns.

Stella Richman's Head of Drama, Peter Wildeblood, though personally charming, was ineffective, and the drama output was not of the best.

Sport was in the hands of Jimmy Hill, who was often photographed in top hat and hunting garb astride some thoroughbred or other. In Company meetings his only topic of conversation was soccer and he would turn any item on the agenda towards his pet subject. So much so that I had a bet with David Gideon Thompson, the Company lawyer, that whatever subject he named I would introduce it and the bet was that however esoteric or off-beat the subject, Jimmy Hill would bring in soccer. So David might give me 'Mathematics' as the question to raise and I would say something on the lines of 'Surely there's a place in our schedule for a popular mathematics series. Perhaps we could acquire the rights of *Mathematics for the Million* and adapt it for tv.' The idea would be discussed and Jimmy Hill would say, 'Yes, maths is important in soccer.' He'd then go into detail about 433 or 244, two sorts of soccer team formations, and I'd have won a pound. Or the subject might be Ancient Greece, and I would raise the possibility of doing an updated version of Aesop's Fables. Jimmy would come in with 'I remember when Fulham played in Greece once; we won 4–0 ...' Another pound to Took.

That was the lighter side of the job. Elsewhere the going was tough. I rationalised, as far as I could, the cumbersome department I'd inherited, sent the really awful producers home (and I'd inherited twenty of varying degrees of ability), persuaded the remainder that better times lay ahead and, in short, did the best with what I was saddled with.

*

One of my biggest headaches was Simon Dee. He'd been headhunted from the BBC by Tito Burns and been made extravagant promises as to what he could do. Dee, who had been a big success as disc jockey and chat show host in BBC TV's *Dee Time*, crossed over to LWT for a late-night chat show called *The Simon Dee Show*. It had started badly and got worse.

It was not a happy show and those involved – researchers Joe Steeples, Patricia Houlihan and Tanya Bruce-Lockart, plus producer Bryan Izzard – seemed ill at ease. Simon Dee was 'difficult', not to say arrogant, and to the unbiased observer *The Simon Dee Show* was pretty poor stuff.

When I arrived at LWT there had already been discussions with Lambeth Palace in which the suggestion had been made that the Archbishop of Canterbury should appear on the show, and one of my first jobs was to indicate to the Archbishop's pushy assistant, who I assumed to be an ambitious, trendy, with-it curate, that to appear for ten minutes in a format that included the Maynard Ferguson Big Band and identical twin sisters, pulchritudinous but dumb, might not be the best platform from which to spread the Christian message. Dee, with justification it must be said, argued that he'd been promised that the Archbishop would appear and failed to see how incongruous it would be.

I compromised and set up a special television recording of a conversation between Dee and the Archbishop that had no other element in it and was transmitted at a different time.

On another occasion the Dee team came to me with the proposition that they should fly to Rome with a camera crew to film an interview with Orson Welles. The Company was very short of money at this time and we were all making what economies we could. To have sent Dee, with his producer, researchers and crew, would have stretched the budget to breaking point. Again I suggested a compromise. I argued that it would be cheaper and just as effective to fly Orson Welles to London, book him a suite at the best hotel, put a chauffeur-driven car at his disposal and conduct the interview in the LWT studios.

At that their enthusiasm for the project waned, but it was that sort of wasteful and unrealistic attitude that had nearly crippled the Company in its early days, and when staff or artists complained that I was cramping their style and that it wasn't like the old days, I pointed out that I was only there because the old days had not proved outstandingly successful.

The real underlying problem with LWT in its early years was the uneasy mix of people from the old Associated Rediffusion and the influx of BBC people. The team of Joy Whitby, Frank Muir and Humphrey Burton, headed by Michael Peacock, expected things to be done the BBC way, while the Rediffusion people had long accepted that in commercial television they were done differently. I'd worked for both sides and had a pretty shrewd idea what was needed and what was possible.

The climax to the Simon Dee saga came when his agent, one of the William Morris Agency staff, told me that Simon might not be able to go on. I said, 'Well, if he is fit and refuses to go on he's breaking his contract', to which this clown from William Morris said, as if producing a trump card, 'But Simon has never signed his contract.' I answered, 'Well, in that case no agreement exists between us and I shall replace him.' The agent huffed and puffed, but seeing that he had painted himself into a corner resorted to reason. 'Simon's a very sensitive person ... the strain of carrying a major show ... feeling disliked by the management ... etc.' So I asked my old friend Pete Murray to stand by to take over if Dee should not appear. Pete understood the situation completely and agreed, and of course on the day Simon Dee turned up and did the show as if nothing had happened. I sent Pete Murray a case of champagne, and soon after, mercifully, Simon Dee finished his series, his contract signed or not was fulfilled and he departed.

I know he felt he'd been badly treated, but I had bigger problems to cope with than him and he was, frankly, a minor irritation.

*

LWT really was in trouble. Financially it was in the soup and there was a considerable feeling in some quarters that it should amalgamate with Thames.

When I joined the Company I was interviewed by Phil Wynn for the Company newspaper, *Weekend News*. He asked, 'Why do you think London Weekend has been criticised so much in the past?' I answered, 'I think the silliest thing this Company did was to put on the play *The Franchise Trail*.'

In this play Nemone Lethbridge told the true story of how the ITA (as the IBA was then known) had been duped into giving the contracts and how the people who had got them were laughing at the stupid old men who had issued those contracts. I told Phil Wynn, 'Anything less likely to make friends and influence people I cannot conceive. It's like a burglar going past the police station and saying to the sergeant, "Oh, by the way, I've just burgled number 27".'

It was clear that the rift between the triumvirate of Chairman Aidan Crawley, Managing Director Tom Margerison and Chief Engineer Vic Gardiner, the remaining member of the old guard, and Stella Richman, was widening. The middle management of the Company kept their heads down, and though Music and Arts, Sport and Children's Programmes were doing well Drama had virtually disappeared and the Light Entertainment department were collectively like the little Dutch boy with his finger in the dyke.

There were other minor irritations, like the time when months in advance I had set up a Christmas Special with the Swingle Singers. The idea was that they should sing, or tootle, or whatever it was that the Swingle Singers did, classical music while on screen we saw a montage of paintings of the Nativity from ancient to modern. It was a neat and inexpensive way to add a Christian note to the Independent Television Christmas of 1970. The man who was responsible for the placing of the programme, Eric Flackfield, breezed into my office one November day and said, 'Oh, I've fixed your *Swingles Sing Christmas* programme.' 'Good,' I said. 'When?' He replied, 'The 5th of February 1971.' My reaction is not repeatable here.

On another occasion the voice of a pushy young man on the phone informed me that he was Jeffrey Archer and that he was organising a charity concert at the Festival Hall featuring Grace Kelly, Frank Sinatra and Bob Hope. For ten thousand pounds we could have the television rights.

It sounded a bargain to me, but Stella Richman scotched it as being too expensive. Ten thousand pounds plus the cost of setting up the outside broadcast was a lot of money in those days, but I felt that such a prestigious line-up would enhance the Company's standing.

Eventually the BBC took on and broadcast the concert. At different times I tried for two shows and was outbidden on both occasions by the BBC – once through the good offices of George Brightwell who, through his association with David Frost, I assumed would help. The show in question was *The Two Ronnies*, who were under some sort of contract to Paradine Productions (a David Frost company), and Brightwell told me I hadn't a hope in hell of getting them as he'd already done a deal with the BBC, in spite of the fact that they'd been appearing regularly on LWT.

The other show I went after was the Tim Brooke-Taylor, Graeme Garden, Bill Oddie combination which Michael Mills snatched and which turned out to be *The Goodies*. Mills argued, quite rightly, that the BBC's facilities for such a programme were infinitely better than LWT's.

Ironically, during my stint as Comedy Adviser to the BBC I had helped a sagging light comedy, *Broaden Your Mind*, starring Brooke-Taylor and Garden, to sharpen up by insisting that they add Oddie to the team. Another irony is that years later when the BBC could no longer afford *The Goodies* it went to LWT.

But in spite of these reverses and frustrations, in the course of 1970 the mood of the Light Entertainment Department had changed.

On the variety side I'd brought in Kenny Everett and Ed 'Stewpot' Stewart, each with his own series, and had set up various specials, one of which starred Dudley Moore and Shari Lewis, who made a delightful couple and a very watchable hour's show. We made a series starring Dickie Henderson, and special programmes of all kinds using what talent was available, including the versatile Reg Varney, impressionist Frank

Gorshin, guitarist John Williams and, on one occasion, Jack Benny.

My inheritance included the successful *Please Sir*, starring John Alderton, *On the Buses* starring Reg Varney, and the slightly rocky Doctor series adapted from the books of Richard Gordon. These were set in hospital and chronicled the antics of the young housemen. Most of the scripts were written by Graham Chapman (between bouts of Pythoning) and Bernard McKenna, and produced by Humphrey Barclay.

I felt it would be better if we sent the star of the show off to General Practice as the aide to an elderly doctor with a pretty daughter. In a phrase that I feel was full of delicacy, nuance and a deep understanding of the psyches of all concerned I said, 'I don't want a load of poofs running around a hospital, I want stories about old ladies with bladder trouble.' And that's what I got, and the ratings soared.

By the highly unorthodox method of colluding with my opposite number at the BBC, Michael Mills, I was able to see that *Please Sir* was not scheduled against *Dad's Army*, but by persuading Mills to tell me what time that excellent Home Guard series was going out (7.30 pm Fridays) I could tell Stella Richman to place *Please Sir* at 8 pm. Thus they didn't clash and those who enjoyed comedy could switch happily from one to the other.

By such ruses and stratagems on one occasion we achieved the remarkable feat of getting both *On the Buses* and *Please Sir* joint top of the ratings.

Morale was high.

We were producing a lot of programmes and coming in under budget. I felt that we ought to try some new ideas – and here I fell flat on my face.

The first of my ghastly mistakes was when I was offered *Sale of the Century*, subsequently a huge success for Anglia Television, with Nicholas Parsons as Chairman. I tried to anglicise it and make it socially aware. As chairman I used Wilfrid Pickles but it was, through no fault of Pickles, a flop and never made it beyond the pilot show. Another quiz which actually did work but never went on the air had some amazing elements, like guessing the nature of objects which the panellists could feel but not see, and other jolly wheezes, but wasn't liked by the management.

Another experiment which was a costly failure and never went on air was a pet project of mine which I called *By Jingo*, a musical history of jingoistic patriotism on the lines of *Oh What a Lovely War*. The research and dialogue were by Penny Chilton, Charles Chilton's wife, and the music by the other half of the successful *Oh What a Lovely War* team, Alf Ralston.

The book was excellent, the musical arrangements perfection and the story followed the rise and fall of patriotic fervour from the Crimean War through the Boer War and World Wars One and Two to Vietnam, and 'Where have all the flowers gone'. Unfortunately it was so badly produced and directed that, much to Stella Richman's dismay, I insisted that we scrap what had been an extremely expensive programme.

I was fortunate in having two assistants, Jon Roseman and Mike Smith, who were both quickwitted and extremely good at figures and understood the needs of any production. Early on in my time with LWT we worked out a cross plot – a sheet of plastic screwed to my office wall on which along one side of a grid were the names of the various shows in production, and at right angles the state of production – e.g. Planning, Budget approved, In rehearsal, Location filming, In studio, Editing, etc. Each day this was updated and we could see at a glance the position of any one programme. It was then easy to calculate how the programme stood as far as budget was concerned and easy for us to shift financial resources around taking from the underspending shows and giving to the programmes needing extra finance – say, for a day lost through rain while on location filming.

It all sounds pretty basic but was the rock on which we built a tight and fiscally accurate method of running the department. At the end of my first year I reckoned that we had produced over three hundred shows and saved 10 per cent of our financial allocation.

It had not been easy, but our successes helped to finance our flops and LE was, by general consent, in better shape than it had ever been.

But under the surface strange things had been happening and dirty doings were afoot. For a start Rupert Murdoch had bought

Lord Weinstock's shares in the company and believed, wrongly, that he now owned LWT.

I had (and have) nothing against Rupert Murdoch. His input into LWT was energetic and far-reaching but almost totally misdirected. By now the management were two opposing camps – pro-Margerison or pro-Richman, with Aidan Crawley, who had in his day been a shrewd and skilful politician but was now an ineffective dodderer, in the middle. During one boardroom row over a vital issue he stopped proceedings to find out the latest score in the test match.

My one meeting with Murdoch was a discussion of the Light Entertainment output. Pointing out the huge audience figures that *On the Buses* was currently receiving, he suggested that we were incompetent by not making more of these money-spinning programmes.

I had to point out that (a) the star, Reg Varney had suffered two minor heart attacks in recent years and overwork might mean a third, which would effectively end the programme; (b) we only had limited studio space, and to add programmes to one series meant dropping them from another, and we had contractual commitments that prevented this; and (c) I personally felt that if we made any more *On the Buses* than we were currently doing we might kill the goose that laid the golden egg.

I think that at first Murdoch was not impressed by my reasoning, thinking it to be some pommy double-talk, but eventually he had to accept the reality of the situation.

*

In early 1971 I had lined up what I thought was an excellent series. An RAF PR man had been to see me to ask if there was any way we could work to our mutual advantage. What we devised was a series of troop concerts in Gibraltar, Malta, Cyprus, the Seychelles and West Germany. The RAF would supply transport for all cast, scenery and technicians free, and we, that is London Weekend, would supply the entertainment. It was a brand-new idea and Stella Richman was enthusiastic. With her entire agreement I contacted Frankie Howerd.

Knowing his record of entertaining the troops all over the world, including the rain forests of Borneo, I felt he was the ideal man for the job. He liked the idea, especially as I had reached an agreement with Ray Galton and Alan Simpson to write the scripts for the shows.

Ray Galton got the picture immediately when I said that one of the locations would be the Seychelles. 'We'll do "Nanook of the North" ' said Ray, 'and Frank can say "The research on this show is terrible." '

There would, of course, be guest artists, a top female singer and well-known actors for the sketch, plus a band, and Frank chatting to the troops and them sending messages home. I even planned to have the Company logo – red, white and blue stripes – filmed in smoke trails by the Red Arrows. It looked good on paper and I sent (courtesy of the RAF), my assistant, Mike Smith, and a senior engineer to recce the locations.

They returned full of enthusiasm, and plans were well advanced when the axe fell. It fell, to my mind wrongly, on Stella Richman, who was forced to go. I found the method and manner of her going despicable and stupid, and without consulting anyone wrote a letter to Crawley, protesting and offering my resignation.

It was accepted and in the brief time I was allowed to clear my desk and leave the building I phoned Harold Davidson, the agent who represented both Kenny Everett and Ed Stewart, to tell him I was going. He apparently phoned Bill Cotton at the BBC, who told Michael Mills, who called David Attenborough who agreed that I should be invited to rejoin the BBC.

Mills then phoned me and we agreed to rendezvous in a pub behind Marble Arch twenty minutes later to discuss the matter.

I then told Lyn what was going on and left LWT for good. Well, not quite as it happens, but more of that later.

In the pub Michael Mills outlined the offer: that I should go back to the BBC as a producer in the Comedy Department. I agreed, with the proviso that I should be allowed to take the training course for directors which would fill a hole in my television education, and the deal was settled then and there. I had been out of work for thirty-five minutes.

When I arrived home later that evening, Lyn greeted me with

the news that not only had the newspapers got the story but other tv companies had too, and I had been offered jobs by both Granada and Yorkshire Television. But by then the die was cast and I'd promised to return to the BBC.

*

My regrets at leaving LWT were mainly that, having begun to build a strong variety department, my work would be quickly undone – as it was. The Howerd venture was cancelled, and it wasn't long before Ed Stewart and Kenny Everett were on the market again.

I'd grown to like the people who worked for LWT – the accountants and studio crews, the production staff and the ladies in the canteen – but my chief regret was parting from my Trinidadian secretary, Theresa Lewis, who had colluded with my wife throughout her time with me and made sure I ate regularly and was spared too many niggling problems. Her one peculiarity was that, coming from a sugar-producing environment, she could not bear artificial sweeteners and when an obliging theatrical agent gave me some new version of saccharine she quietly disposed of them and went back to putting sugar in my coffee.

I'd inaugurated shows, made money for the company, bolstered morale, carried the can for flops, made friends for life with some people and earned undying enmity from others. I'd worked a twelve-hour day, seven days a week, and learnt a lot.

I never managed to solve the problem of putting Kenny Everett on the screen effectively. That was done some years later by Thames Television. I'd worked for what I believe was the most obtuse management in the history of British television … and I've worked for them all. Crawley, the Chairman, was ineffective. Tom Margerison was a Svengali who unfortunately hadn't got a Trilby to sing to him. Vic Gardiner was an engineer who thought he was a showman and, although good as the former, was hopeless as the latter.

Murdoch's influence was shortlived, but in his brief, whirlwind stay with the company he ditched not only Stella Richman but also Margerison and Crawley shortly after.

My replacement was Michael Grade. Michael had until then been an agent and is the son of an agent, the late Leslie Grade, brother of Lew Grade and Bernard Delfont. But while both Lew and Bernard became life peers, poor old Leslie didn't get so much as a British Empire Medal, and when he died his estate was valued at £400.

No doubt, shrewd man that he was, he made sure that little was left for death duties. Michael, like his father, is astute and a sharp businessman, but unlike his father he is easily bored and tends to tantrums. On one occasion when he didn't get his own way he threw the telephone out of his Regent Street office window. On another, representing Leslie Crowther who was headlining a series for LWT, he became displeased with some aspect of the show and screamed abuse and recrimination at all and sundry.

I'd just started, the show was new to me and I was taken aback. In a second Leslie Crowther series I engaged the toughest producer/director I knew, William G. Stewart, with instructions that, should Michael Grade become difficult, he was to be quietly but firmly chucked out of the studio. Fortunately the situation never arose.

Michael Grade was a good choice as Head of Light Entertainment at London Weekend as his contacts and knowledge of the variety scene were invaluable. He subsequently became Programme Controller, left to run his own company in the USA and, when that folded, returned to the UK and the job of Controller of Programmes for BBC 1.

It was a move that surprised nearly everybody, but it was no surprise to me when he left the BBC abruptly after only a few months and took over the running of Channel 4. Michael Grade is a man of mercurial temperament and by the time this book is published I would not be surprised to hear that he is working somewhere else.

*

The postscript to my sojourn at LWT came some years later when they were in dispute with British Actors Equity over the use of non-union performers. It was a series where amateur joke-tellers told jokes they'd probably heard from their professional counterparts. Equity objected on the ground that it was depriving their members of gainful employment. The dispute went to a tribunal under the guidance of Diana Cotton QC. Michael Grade asked me to fight LWT's case and John Morton of the Musicians Union spoke for Equity. It came out a draw. LWT withdrew the programme and Equity took no punitive action. As in all draws, no one was happy with the result, but at least no one lost.

Today LWT is well run, has an excellent management and is very profitable. In 1970 it was like standing on the sloping deck of the sinking Titanic while the Palm Court orchestra played 'In the Shadows'.

13

Back at the Beeb

On my return to the warm embrace of the BBC I found the atmosphere calm and relaxed after the ceaseless hubbub of LWT and I quickly settled back into the routine of being a BBC man again.

One of the most interesting things I did in 1971 was a radio series called *The Best of British Laughter* in which, week by week, I interviewed Benny Hill, Peter Sellers, Morecambe and Wise, Ken Dodd and Ted Ray, and for the sixth in the series edited and presented a composite programme called *The Goons to Monty Python*. The producer was John Browell. Interviewing Ted Ray, Benny Hill and Morecambe and Wise in a studio at Broadcasting House was straightforward and uncomplicated, as was the compilation programme, but Ken Dodd and Peter Sellers were a different proposition.

Ken Dodd was appearing as Malvolio in *Twelfth Night* in Liverpool and couldn't get to London. But he could make it to Manchester, and thither John Browell and I hied ourselves for the recording in the BBC Manchester studios. I'd prepared a list of questions and Ken Dodd duly arrived and we started to record. My first question was 'How did you start in show business?' Ken Dodd told me, amplified his answer, developed his theme and told anecdotes of his career. After thirty minutes John Browell signalled to me from the control room that time was up. I thanked Ken for being so forthcoming, and that was it. I had nodded and smiled for thirty minutes, but apart from introducing the programme and signing off I hadn't said a word.

With Peter Sellers it was different. At that time he was living in Maynooth in Eire, separated from his then wife, Miranda Quarrie, and had rented or bought the greater part of a castle where, with his cars and stereo equipment for company, he was living as a tax exile. John Browell had been, in years past, one of the most successful of the *Goon Show* producers, and Peter Sellers had readily agreed to the interview when John had phoned him. However, when we arrived, after flying from Heathrow to Dublin, and then travelling by road in a rickety taxi from the airport to Meynooth, he had decided that perhaps he didn't want to be interviewed after all.

John Browell, who was subject to fierce migraine headaches, was shattered by this news and went into a pretty bad spasm barely able to hear, see or speak.

Sellers was very concerned and, once we had propped John Browell in a fairly comfortable position, said, 'Look, I'll work the recorder, you hold the mike and we'll talk.'

And talk we did: about Sellers's career on radio, in films, and on the stage. It was a good, meaty interview, and by the time we'd used up all the tape John had come round and was feeling much better. He was quite distressed still, but we assured him that he *did* have a programme after all, and he and I returned to London much happier than we'd been some hours earlier.

It's a sad thought that Peter Sellers had given so few interviews in his lifetime that our Meynooth recording was extensively used in obituary programmes when he died. It was one of the few occasions when, in public, he'd owned up.

Sellers said, in effect: 'I don't exist. I only come to life as the character I'm playing. When I'm not in character I become bewildered, ill at ease and behave foolishly. Harry Secombe has his singing to fall back on, Spike Milligan has his writing. I have nothing.'

I think it was this strong feeling that he had no identity of his own which led Sellers into so many disasters both in marriage and on the screen.

*

By March 1971 I had a lot of work on my plate. At the BBC Television Centre Michael Mills was planning to produce Evelyn

Waugh's *Scoop* for the screen and asked me to do the adaptation.

Besides that I spent much of April putting together a lecture to be given, jointly with Michael Mills, at the 1971 Montreux Light Entertainment Festival.

Michael spoke first, talking from the producers' point of view, and I followed, speaking for the writers. It was a variation on lectures we'd given in other places, notably Dublin, and had usually gone well.

On this occasion, however, Michael spoke in with such arrogant assurance ('British television is best, and the BBC is the better of the UK networks, and comedy is king ...') that the crowd of practitioners from every country in Europe got its collective back up and Michael was greeted with rumblings of disapproval from East (USSR, Czechoslovakia, etc) and West (France, Spain, Germany and the rest).

When it came to my turn to speak they were more like a lynch mob than an audience and I took a much more placatory tone than I had intended. The rumblings of revolution died away and we finished the conference with an exchange of views (the multi-lingual interpreters working overtime) that was both constructive and satisfactory. As a result I was asked to speak at a seminar in Denmark later that year, attended by all the Scandinavian tv companies, and later still in Finland at a symposium to do with humour in children's television.

That Montreux gathering had teetered on the brink of disaster, though, and I was glad that, in the end, we had got away with it.

Mills, who could be brilliant, could also be obtuse and objectionable. The previous year, while I was still with LWT, we had gone at the invitation of a Dr Biolek to Munich to talk about Comedy to the West German television people.

Here too Michael adopted a belligerent tone and I can remember clearly sitting at one end of a long dinner table in a Munich restaurant, where we were being entertained by our hosts, talking soccer, and in particular the merits of the German centre forward, Uwe Seeler: a fairly anodyne subject. We were there, after all, to sell tv programmes to Germany and not fight World War Two all over again. But Michael with, as the Irish would say, 'a drop taken', was holding forth about his time at a

German university in the 30s. Loud and clear his voice rang through the restaurant: 'Well, I was here in 1938 and *I* knew what was going on.'

And, speaking of the Irish, on our visit to Dublin boosting BBC Comedy, Tom Sloan, Michael Mills and I did our stuff, the Irish were charm itself and the visit was a useful piece of PR. In those days the BBC could seem extremely arrogant and self-satisfied and our trip was a useful piece of bridge-building between BBC and Radio Telefis Eireann. For Michael Mills, however, the trip was something of a nightmare as, everywhere we went, or so it seemed, whether to pub, hotel or restaurant, a passing drunk would vomit over him. Sloan and I took to keeping well away from Mills, for without fail as we were entering one or another of the establishments we visited on our trip to Dublin some poor soul was on his way out to pay his respects to the Liffey and never seemed to be able to make it in time.

At his best Mills was a genius, making successes where no other producer – with the possible exception of that other eccentric, Dennis Main Wilson – would have made anything of a project. At his worst, and we'll come to *Scoop* in due course, he was an absolute menace.

Looking back, I'm reminded of an expression of my father's: 'You may be a joy to your mother but you're a pain in the neck to me.' And it must be said that in his erratic and traumatic career Michael Mills was either loved or loathed. If pressed, I'd admit that in spite of his many foibles I was extremely fond of him and miss him greatly.

*

After the Montreux trip my next big project was working on George Schlatter's tv spectacular, *It's a Wacky World*. George, my old boss from *Laugh In*, had planned a multi-national comedy with funny people from all over contributing. It was full of *Laugh In* type slapstick jokes and featured such people as John Cleese, Tony Curtis, Elke Sommer, Sheldon Leonard, Alfonso Aral (in Mexico), a Swedish tumbling act called The Stupids, me acting in bit-parts and looking after some of the finances as associate producer, and Jacques Tati.

NUTS — BT as TV Presenter (1977)

Left to right: My Father, Uncle Roland, Aunt Olive, Aunt Lilian, Uncle Alfred and Aunt Florence (1936)

The Took family — Father, Mother, Number One Son, and Nurse holding 'Euston' (June 1928)

Philip, Mother and me (1929)

'The Age of Innocence'.
BT aged 17 (1945)

'Legitimate at last'. Lyn and me on our wedding day (29 October 1965)

'I expect you're wondering why I sent for you' (1955)

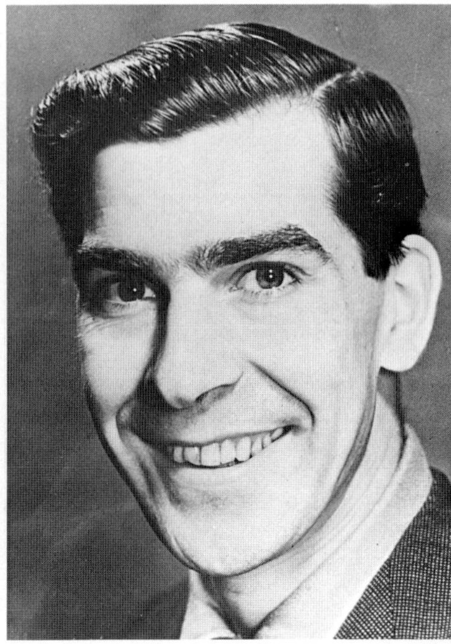

For Amusement Only (1956)

It's A Pleasure — RAF Gloucester (1948). Left to right: BT, Frank McDonnell, Geoffrey Flowerdew, Dai Francis, John Martindale.

'Too sophisticated for tea?' On tour (1952)

BT beginning to make a name for himself (1953)

The song that returned to haunt me (1956)

Beyond Our Ken: 1st series (1958/59). Left to right from the back: Kenneth Williams, Ron Moody, Hugh Paddick, Betty Marsden, Kenneth Horne, Pat Lancaster, BT, Eric Merriman.

LICENSED ANNUALLY BY THE LONDON COUNTY COUNCIL. MEMBERS OF THE AGENTS' ASSOCIATION LIMITED.

REGISTERED OFFICE: 52, JERMYN ST. LONDON, S.W.1.

Associated London Scripts Limited

Managing Director:
STANLEY DALE
12, Holland Villas Road,
Kensington,
London, W.14.
PARK 4201

Please reply to
Cumberland House

General Manager:
MRS BERYL VERTUE
2, Cumberland House,
Kensington High Street,
London, W.8.
WESTERN 8274

1st July 1959

Barry Took Esq.,
6, Creighton Avenue,
London, N.10.

Dear Barry,

Peter Eton has been on to me as he particularly wants to see you this week to discuss the possibility of you as a regular in the "Army Game" (again!). I told him I thought this would be very doubtful in view of your writing comitments, but he had heard a rumour that "Take It From Here" was perhaps unlikely, and was, therefore, asking you again. Regarding this rumour, having heard it from another source as well, I checked with the B.B.C. but they said although there had been a "little trouble", everybody was signed and the series was on.

I told Peter Eton this, but he still wants to see you, and to keep on the right side of everybody, I think it would be a good thing if you give him a ring.

I am going on holiday on Friday evening, but please ring me at home on Thursday afternoon or the office on Friday morning.

Luv,

Beryl

DIRECTORS:- STANLEY DALE (MANAGING). RAY GALTON. TONY HANCOCK. FRANKIE HOWERD. SPIKE MILLIGAN. ALAN SIMPSON (CHAIRMAN). ERIC SYKES.

The 'little trouble' Beryl Vertue mentions in her letter meant the end of one writing partnership and the start of another.

Three comedy writers (BT, Alan Simpson and Ray Galton) making each other laugh for a change (1972)

LWT
London Weekend Television

South Bank Television Centre, Kent House, Upper Ground, London SE1 9LT. (Registered Office)
Telex: 918123. Cables: Weekendtel London SE1. PBX Telephone: 01-261 3434.

Direct Line: 01-261 3040

Barry Took, Esq.,
17, Hanover House,
St. John's Wood High Street,
London N.W.8.

28th November 1978

Dear Barry,

I really would like to record my sincere thanks to you for all the efforts you made at the recent Arbitration. I am personally most grateful.

Kindest regards.

Yours sincerely,

Michael Grade
Director of Programmes

c.c. Thanks for the tip about those young writers. Humphrey is following it up.

London Weekend Television Limited. Registered in England (No. 908673)
Directors: John Freeman CHAIRMAN, Lord Hartwell DEPUTY CHAIRMAN, Brian Tesler MANAGING DIRECTOR, Vic Gardiner GENERAL MANAGER, Michael Grade DIRECTOR OF PROGRAMMES, Ron Miller SALES DIRECTOR, Peter McNally FINANCIAL DIRECTOR, G.H. Ross Goobey, H.C. Hardy, Roger Harrison, Duncan McNab, The Hon. David Montagu, Evelyn de Rothschild.

Those 'young writers' were Laurence Marks and Maurice Gran, now among Britain's highest paid script writers, with TV hits *Shine On Harvey Moon*, *Roll Over Beethoven*, *The New Statesman* and *Birds Of A Feather* to their credit. The Humphrey mentioned is Humphrey Barclay, the TV producer.

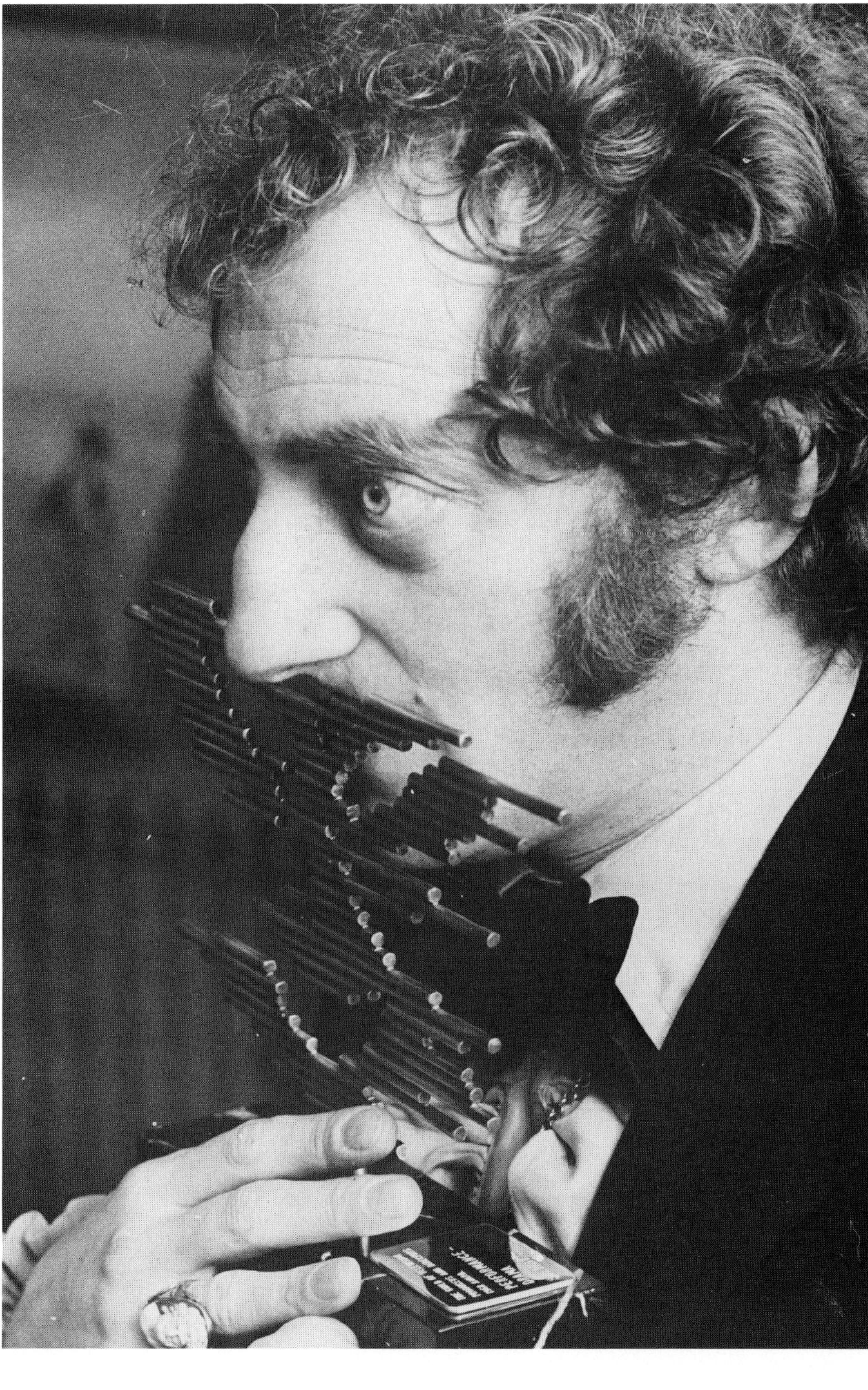

Marty Feldman looking sombre on the night of Kenneth Horne's death, during the BAFTA Awards of 1969.

ALBSU
Adult Literacy & Basic Skills Unit
FOOTBALL
I'LL PLAY AGAIN FOR ENGLAND
Time for a few home tru
POOR HODDLE—HO
Barry Took says:
"GET HELP NOW!
Learn to read and write better"

On the Move

Ernie Wise getting the laughs (1987)

Took & Co (YTV). Left to right: Gwen Taylor, David Battley, Robin Bailey, Chris Emmett and Andrew Sachs (1978)

Mrs Thatcher, visiting the BBC, is slightly overcome by the awesome majesty of it all. BT does his impersonation of a Victorian curate (1980)

The Flook Squad. BT, Trog (Wally Fawkes), Barry Norman and George Melly (1975)

Attempting to amuse the Television Industry, with Mrs Brian Tesler (on my left) wincing at a joke (1983)

BT with Michael Palin of Arabia (actually during filming of *Life of Brian* in Tunisia) (1978)

Being 'didactic' — lecturing in Australia (1984)

Six faces of Took (1990)

A tasteful moment, with *News Quiz* stalwarts Alan Coren, John Wells and Richard Ingrams (1989)

The ace in the pack was Jacques Tati, and George Schlatter really needed him in the show to give it both an international star name and a 'first', as Tati had never appeared in an American tv special.

So George Schlatter and I went to Paris to meet the great French comedian. George announced on our way over that he'd never seen any Tati films but that his deal with NBC would only be confirmed if Tati signed.

I briefed George, and George using my briefing as a back-up to his own powers of persuasion was a pretty sensational salesman. Tati duly agreed to do the show. George and I returned to England to shoot scenes in and around London, while Tati took a week in Trouville to improve his complexion.

Getting back to England from Paris wasn't that easy. It was Whitsun and all Air France flights were full. I got us onto a standby list with British Airways and we finally did get seats, but not before the French stewardess in charge of the boarding arrangements misread my name as Toole rather than Took, and all over Orly Airport the message boomed 'Will Monsieur Toole report to desk 23'.

George was rather taken with this, and as recently as 1989 when I phoned him in LA he greeted me cheerily with 'Ah, Monsieur Toole, how good to hear from you'.

*

Back in London we filmed a sequence where John Cleese and I, dressed as typical English businessmen – bowler hats, black coats, striped trousers and old school ties – are taking tea at a pavement café (off Curzon Street) as a pretty girl walks by. We are unmoved by this (so went the scenario) but the sight arouses the Latin blood of the waiter who, while pouring tea, follows the pretty girl with his eyes and pours the scalding hot tea into the laps of the businessmen.

George booked a *real* waiter to do the pouring, and we rehearsed (without the props) with me holding a bucket between my legs to receive the tea and acting the part of a man with scalded private parts. For the take the restaurant had thoughtfully provided a teapot of the type used in mass catering and filled it with genuinely hot tea. The director, Ian McNaughton, shouted 'action'. John Cleese and I chatted, the pretty girl walked by, the waiter turned to follow her and poured the scalding hot tea into my lap, missing the waiting bucket by a good ten inches. I didn't act the role of a man scalded in his private parts, I *was* that man. It was fairly painful but, old ham that I was, I stuck it out till the director shouted 'Cut', and then screamed with agony.

Fortunately the trousers I was wearing were made of pretty thick material and thus total disaster was averted, but when both tea and I had cooled down and the crew prepared for further shots that didn't require me in them I was at liberty to walk to Grosvenor House in Park Lane, where a temporary HQ had been set up, soaked from the waist down in brown fluid. It says much for the Shepherd Market haberdashers that the assistant didn't turn a hair when I crept, crab-like, into his shop and asked to purchase one pair of underpants. He sold them to me without a flicker of surprise on his face and bowed me gravely out into the street. I scuttled to Grosvenor House and changed. It is not an experience I would like to repeat.

Another incident comes to mind: George trying to persuade Laurence Olivier to appear in 'a cameo', that's to say a walk-on part. The production team were gathered in George's hotel suite when his call to Olivier's office was returned.

'Can I speak with Laurence Olivier.'

'It's *Sir* Laurence,' Assistant Producer Carolyn Raskin hissed.

Before I could correct her, Olivier's office did.

'He's a what?' said George, 'A *Lord*! How come?'

He cupped his hand over the phone and turned to the rest of us with a huge grin. 'How do you like that – he's been *elevated*!'

Needless to say Lord Olivier declined George's offer of a walk-on part in *It's a Wacky World*.

*

A week later we were back in Paris ready to film Tati.

The setting was the Café de Flore in the Boulevard St Germain, which had been rented for the morning, and where

Tati was to play a clumsy waiter upsetting the entire clientele. The extras were in place at the café tables, the German film crew were in position, and a second crew (a German news unit who happened to be in town and had been co-opted by our director, Michael Pfleger) had taken up their position at a window above the Brasserie Lipp across the road.

The only thing missing was the star. Of Jacques Tati there was no sign, and as 10 am approached Schlatter and his aides started to get anxious. Suppose he didn't turn up?

Well, eventually he did arrive, an hour later, in a small car, which he parked with a flourish. He got out, bowed to the ladies in the group and then went into a huddle with Schlatter, Carolyn Raskin, who had joined us in Paris for the shoot, and various other members of the entourage.

After a few moments, Carolyn Raskin detached herself from the crowd around Tati and came over to where I was chatting with a member of the German crew. She said, 'Barry, what's five million lire in dollars?' I said, 'Why do you ask?' She said, 'Well, that's what Tati wants for the day's shooting.'

I took out my pen and searched my pockets for some paper on which I could make the calculation required. I couldn't find any, so I did the sums on the trunk of a convenient plane tree, converting lire into pounds and pounds into dollars. It wasn't a vast amount of money and Tati wanted it in lire paid into an Italian bank because at the time he was an undischarged bankrupt in France.

This, incidentally, was not a novel situation for him as his films were almost always wildly over budget and, until they earned money from overseas sales, Tati was broke. The five million lire fee was quickly agreed,and at last filming started.

At lunchtime we departed for a Paris film studio to complete the day's shooting on an outdoor set that duplicated a corner of the Café de Flore. Unfortunately in mid-afternoon it started to rain and filming had to stop. We all adjourned to the small studio bar, which was full of other actors and technicians who had also been rained off.

I found myself next to Tati. I bought him a cup of coffee and we started talking. It was quite amicable until I mentioned that I knew Marcel Marceau slightly. Tati bristled. How could I compare that Mime and his unchanging repertoire with him, Jacques Tati, the great creative artiste. I protested that I wasn't comparing them, but merely saying that each was great in his own way.

Tati persisted in his criticism of Marceau and our conversation became quite heated. Looking round, I saw to my surprise Jean Paul Belmondo and Omar Sharif standing open-mouthed, listening.

Eventually Tati ended what had by now become an argument by saying, 'But what do you know? You are only an accountant.'

Admittedly I was wearing a grey suit, white shirt and sober tie, but I was returning to London later that afternoon for an interview at the BBC. I protested that in spite of appearances I was not an accountant but a writer and associate producer on the *Wacky World* project. Tati was not convinced. He said, 'You *are* an accountant and there is a tree in the Boulevard St Germain that can prove it.'

*

Fortunately the rain stopped then and they got on with the filming while I returned to England to make a documentary, based vaguely on my early music hall days, in the small town of Holmfirth in Yorkshire.

Actually the producer, Michael Raybiger, and I had planned to go to Blythe in Northumberland but the theatre was shut as, it appeared, was most of the town, and we decided to look elsewhere. In covering the Huddersfield/Halifax area of Yorkshire we stumbled upon Holmfirth and decided it was the ideal spot to make a film. At that time, 1971, it was only known for Bamforths, the picture-postcard company, who had incidentally made a foray into the field of film production before World War One. The weather had defeated them. Otherwise, had they had Californian sunshine in the shadow of the Pennines, Britain might have a thriving film industry today.

Holmfirth is now known as the location for the highly successful tv series *Last of the Summer Wine*, but then it was virtually unknown.

Our film covered Bamforths and its story, the local brass band, the working men's club with its Sunday lunchtime strip show, and interviews with various residents and people who worked in the local woollen industry.

One of these men, a dyer, confessed that he'd only been to London once in his life and that was when he passed through the capital on his way home after demob from the army in 1945.

That interview and the fact that we hadn't filmed the new fire station, the pride and joy of the town, brought angry reactions on the lines of 'Took made us look like ignorant provincials'. That wasn't the point at all. What had impressed me was that the dyer, and in fact almost everyone we met in Holmfirth seemed so contented with their lot that they didn't need the spurious excitements of the South of England.

I saw Holmfirth as a rather chilly garden of Eden, and it was, as it turned out, just that quality of innocence and tranquillity that gave *Last of the Summer Wine* its special flavour.

My Holmfirth stint, which was part of a series called *Six Characters in Search of* ... wasn't my first documentary that year. In April I filmed an episode of *One Man's Week* which, being not unlike another series looking at individuals' reactions to their own lives called *One Pair of Eyes*, I christened *One Man's Weak Pair of Eyes*. (I'd always had a fancy for fooling around with names and titles: thus Una Stubbs had become Eunice Tubbs and the Granada tv music series *Spot the Tune* became *Tune up Your Spots*.)

One Man's Week consisted of my chatting to Ned Sherrin – whose life must seem bound to mine, so often do I mention him, but whom I hardly know. All I do know is that he was a good friend when I fell on hard times or was emotionally bruised by events, and while today I don't regard him quite as the genius I once did, he has a formidable talent and is excellent company if you're in the mood for a gossip. Others I chatted to were Peter Black, the tv critic, and Philip Oakes, the poet, novelist and journalist. Peter Black was one of the founders of an informal luncheon club that had assembled in Montreux for the Festival of Light Entertainment every spring. The second member was Philip Purser, tv critic of the *Sunday Telegraph*. The third member was Leonard Marsland Gander, the doyen of the critics, having been the first serious television critic (for the *Daily*

Telegraph), and I was the fourth.

In spite of his advanced years and wide experience, Leonard Marsland Gander was a great romantic and saw in the most mundane events inspirational or tender scenes.

At one dinner, noticing that our waitress had a rather pronounced bulge under her short apron, Marsland Gander launched into the speculation that this girl, this child of the mountains, had in the careless rapture of spring been indiscreet with a passing goatherd and had come to Montreux to earn a little money and have her child in the anonymity of the city before returning to her village where her shame would never be known. This simple earth mother touched Marsland Gander's finest impulses, and with every new order of beer or food he would pay the bill and tip her lavishly, saying as he did so, 'She needs our help.'

I forget who it was at the table who pointed out that, far from pregnancy being the cause of the bulge under the apron, that was where the waitress kept her purse, where she put the money she was given and from which she dispensed change. Marsland Gander's largesse had perceptibly increased the bulge during our meal. He saw the point but insisted that he preferred his version.

In the four years I went to Montreux – 1969, '70, '71 and '72 – our quartet never failed to meet, chat and laugh. They, of course, had to file copy while I was, in theory at least, on the other, or tv programme making, side. That they accepted me as one of them was heartening because it must be said that tv people en masse are excruciatingly boring. My first visit to Montreux was as co-writer of *Marty*, the BBC's entry. My second was as London Weekend's Head of Light Entertainment. My third was, as I have already described, as the guest of the organisers to deliver a lecture, and my fourth, yet to come in this narrative, was to collect material for a book (never written) which was to be the tv companion to my history of radio comedy – *Laughter in the Air*.

*

In June 1971 I settled down to the first important piece of literary adaptation I'd ever tackled, Evelyn Waugh's *Scoop*.

Michael Mills had resigned as Head of Comedy at the BBC to concentrate on what he really enjoyed, producing. In years to come his credits in this field would include *Clochemerle* (adapted by Ray Galton and Alan Simpson), *Some Mothers Do 'Ave 'Em*, starring Michael Crawford, and *Chance in a Million* for Thames TV, which starred Simon Callow and Brenda Blethyn. *Scoop* was to be his first venture back in producer's harness, and I was to turn it into seven thirty-minute episodes.

The reason Mills was so keen on making *Scoop* was that he had heard that Paramount Pictures were planning a version of the book, starring Harry Worth, and he went to great lengths to get in first, securing the rights to the book and signing the actor.

I had my doubts. Surely the hero of the book was a young, shy man in his teens. Wasn't Harry Worth too old? Mills brushed aside my doubts assuring me that the well-known and very popular dithering character of Harry Worth was exactly what was required to ensure that *Scoop* reached the large audience it deserved.

I shrugged and pressed on. To my mind the first rule of adaptation is to be entirely faithful to the book. That is, of course, as far as the text is concerned. The visual interpretation of the events calls for imagination and ingenuity, but provided the cast are adequate and the producer sensitive what can go wrong?

In the case of *Scoop*, practically everything. Because Harry Worth was obviously middle-aged, the girl friend couldn't be a teenager or he'd have looked – that is, the character Boot would have looked – like a dirty old man. Sinead Cusack was booked, who though certainly not middle-aged was mature enough for us to get over that hurdle. But it did mean that William Boot's elderly relatives had to be *really* elderly, and elderly actors tend to deliver their lines slowly (as indeed they should), but this means that short scenes become long and long scenes become interminable.

Mills's obsession with accuracy now meant that as scenes in the African capital of Ishmalia were in the rainy season the studio sets would have water pouring down on them. Not the *effect* of rain but real water pumping up over the sets and released like proper rain, which would then drain into special troughs and be recycled.

This was extremely noisy, the cast had to shout in order to convey anything to each other and the studio audience couldn't hear a word.

Yes, we had a studio audience who, not knowing the story and expecting the Harry Worth they knew from previous series of broad situation comedy, were utterly baffled.

Some scenes worked well and the location filming (in the home counties, but mercifully not Africa) was good, but the whole was not equal to the sum of its parts and *Scoop* was a resounding flop.

I had foreseen this and had gone to the new Head of Comedy, Duncan Wood, with the proposition that if he cancelled the series I would not only refund the script fees but write a replacement series free.

Events were too far advanced for that to be a possibility and in fact the first press reactions were good.

Here's Peter Black on the subject:

> With a favourite book one's ear is always alert for calamitous false notes, but I don't see how Barry Took could have done it better. The extra jokes were stylishly in harmony with the original ... Harry's performance was more exactly right than anyone except Brian Oulton's as Mr Slater, the much abused editor of *The Daily Beast*.

I suppose, looking back with all passion spent, *Scoop* can go down as a brave try, and in fact the difficulty of turning that particular book into a television play was illustrated nearly twenty years later when London Weekend Television had a (very expensive) go at it, and muffed it completely.

Though I adapted the novel in 1971, *Scoop* didn't go out until 1972, and the rest of '71 was a comparatively quiet time for me.

*

My next major project was to write (with others) and direct a late night Intimate Revue at the Hampstead Theatre Club, starring the transvestite Comedians Rogers and Starr. This went into production in 1972 and I had just one big show left to do in '71, *The Private Eye Revue*.

I'd been trying to interest people both at the BBC and LWT for three years in the idea of televising *Private Eye*, and now with the tenth anniversary of the satirical magazine coming up it seemed time to have another go. Huw Wheldon, the Managing Director of BBC TV, had vetoed earlier approaches on the grounds that a *Private Eye* programme would be obscene and libellous.

I wrote a script on spec to prove that it needn't be either, the BBC were won over and I was duly commissioned. Dennis Main Wilson became the producer, and the show was made on 23 December 1971.

So, a year that had started gloomily finished on a high note, and Lyn and I saw the old year out looking back over 'what might have been' with regret, but forward to a future that looked – well, promising.

14

Down and Out

The most important event for me in 1972 was the news that not only was I broke but I owed the Inland Revenue vast sums of money.

Without whining it must be said that I'd been badly let down by a large firm of accountants who seemed to specialise in letting down members of the theatrical profession; but thanks to a decent and understanding bank manager, a Mr Bannister (whom God preserve) of the National Westminster who introduced us to the accountants Malvern and Co., Lyn and I were saved from utter bankruptcy, and Ronnie Malvern helped us put our house in order and passed us on eventually to one of his bright young men, Richard Goldman, who has looked after our financial affairs ever since and is beyond praise both as friend and accountant.

The immediate effect of the 1972 financial debacle however was that we had no money at all, apart from my smallish BBC salary and whatever else I could legitimately pick up outside. Which brings me to Rogers and Starr.

Their real names are Michael Rogers and Roy Starling, and by day they were window-dressers. By night, however, they dressed in women's clothes and did the funniest camp drag act I'd ever seen. I first saw them in action in some tatty concert room in 1969 and was so impressed with their exquisite costumes and irreverent rudery that I filmed them at Thames during my time as producer of *Horne A' Plenty*.

The act didn't work on television; it was designed for cabaret and the sort of pub concert that flourished in the late sixties and early seventies. In 1971 Michael, Roy and I met again. Harold Fielding, the impresario, had invited them to do a late night revue after the main attraction at the Hampstead Theatre Club and they asked me if I would write and direct it.

Of course they had quite a lot of material of their own, in particular a hilariously filthy version of The Lady of Shallot, but would obviously need more numbers and a supporting cast to fill the hour required.

I was intrigued because not only did I regard them as excellent entertainers but I'd never directed in the theatre before and had written very little revue material.

A deal was struck. A cast – Antonia Ellis, Ray Davis and Paul McDowell – were booked, and I commissioned material from N.F. Simpson, Michael Palin, Terry Jones and Paul McDowell; and from Geoff Rowley and Andy Baker who were two young writers from Stockport I'd discovered while working at Thames and had put under contract when I was at London Weekend Television.

The balance of the show, which I called *Handy for the Heath* – a line taken from an estate agent's handout – I wrote myself. A dear friend, Malcolm Clare, was the choreographer, and Ronnie Cass wrote the music.

After a few weeks of tough rehearsal we opened on 26 January 1972, and *Handy for the Heath* was an enormous success for Rogers and Starr. It's true that they brought a large contingent of their supporters with them, but the show was taut, fast-moving and funny. It was scheduled for a month and it became clear early on that as the first month was a sell-out a second edition should be put into commission to follow the first.

For this four-week run Derek Griffiths replaced Paul McDowell, and in addition to what I wrote new material came from Donald Churchill.

B.A. Young, writing in the *Financial Times* said:

> In this second edition of the Rogers and Starr show, Barry Took's direction has welded a welcome touch of professionalism to the intransigent amateurism that is part of Rogers and Starr's armament ... I'm not sure if Derek Griffiths' mime of a careless surgeon in the operating theatre isn't the best thing of the evening, though Antonia Ellis' Netherlands Song for Eurovision ('In my little dutch cap with my finger in a dyke') runs it close.

> Rogers and Starr establish intimate terms with their audience as soon as they make their first entrance, and their audience isn't by any means the kind of Gay Lib crowd you might imagine ... The current revue is often hilariously funny ... pretty to look at [and] I was reminded of the days when revue was still a fine art.

So big was the applause at the end of the show that it was imperative to write an encore number. Ronnie Cass and I came up with the following. The whole idea seems terribly dated now, but the number, sung in the manner of a barbershop quartet, still has a touch of the wry humour that brought the house down in 1972.

Don't Drop the Bomb on Hampstead

Verse

Mr Kosygin, Mr Nixon, Chairman Mao,
We've a little message, so listen now.
If your urge to drop the H bomb
Is really hot
Then just go ahead and do it,
But avoid one spot
We beg you ...

Chorus

Don't drop the bomb on Hampstead,
Don't drop the bomb, I pray.
If you should unleash your appliances,
Just think of what folk would say.
Intellectual life in Hampstead
Is, in a word, unique,
And if you dropped the bomb on Hampstead
You'd put culture back nearly a week.

2nd Chorus

Don't drop the bomb on Hampstead,
Heed my sincere advice.
Think of the woe you'd be bound to cause
If you explode your device.
The people of happy Hampstead
Could scarcely be happy dead,
So please don't drop the bomb on Hampstead –
Drop it on Highgate instead ...
Or Camden Town.

The success of *Handy for the Heath* was such that Harold Fielding decided to transfer it to the West End. But I was dropped, along with the material I'd assembled, with the exception of one brilliant sketch by Donald Churchill about a married couple in bed trying to fantasise themselves back to ardour by imagining their partner was someone else.

Michael Rogers and I had fallen out, due to some trivial misunderstanding, and he showed a blazing bitchiness I hadn't suspected before. Roy was quiet and remained uninvolved, but that was the end of our relationship. For some obscure reason Fielding set the London version of the show in a public lavatory, and brought in Jimmy Edwards, who had recently confessed his homosexual leanings. The sketches and songs in the new show were pretty dreadful and the Criterion Theatre, though small by West End standards, was too big for Rogers and Starr's intimate brand of comedy. The show staggered along for a few weeks before collapsing. Michael Rogers went to the States and Roy Starr went back to window-dressing.

What B.A. Young had called their 'intransigent amateurism' had been their undoing. It was a pity, for they were both nice people and didn't deserve what they got at the Criterion.

So much for the theatre. Television is much safer.

*

My first tv series as a BBC producer was to star Sheila Hancock, and we met early in 1972 to discuss it.

Sheila was in a fairly gloomy frame of mind as she had recently lost her mother and her husband, who had both died of cancer. She didn't want a purely funny show but something with a bite to it.

The formula we came up with, a combination of chat show and sketch-and-song comedy, we called *But Seriously – It's Sheila Hancock*. We made six programmes, each one with a theme and each with one or more guest stars.

Sheila, as I say, was extremely depressed, and her attitude was 'I know you won't be able to get me so-and-so', but as it happened I got her every so-and-so she asked for: Germaine Greer, Dudley Moore, Peter Hall, Peter Jones, John Mortimer, Michael Hordern, John Bird, Anthony Hopkins the musicologist, and Kenneth Allsop, who was a guest in an edition about Ecology. The subjects we tackled were Women's Lib, the Law,

Music (a programme in which Dudley Moore and Anthony Hopkins argued as to who was the shorter of the two), the Theatre: a programme in which Peter Hall accepted the small fee we offered but stipulated that a chauffeur-driven Rolls Royce must collect him and take him home after the recording.

The Women's Lib programme, naturally enough, was the one featuring Germaine Greer, and we sent Sheila and Germaine to a West End sex shop to buy various items and discuss them on the programme.

Getting wind of this, the editor of the *Radio Times*, Geoffrey Cannon, said that if I put that programme out first of the six he would commission Ray Connolly to write an article about it, which would be complemented by several colour photographs. I knew this would please Sheila, but I wasn't prepared for the flak I got from the 6th floor of the TV Centre. Huw Wheldon had hated the programme, and even my friend David Attenborough had found it tasteless and unnecessarily provocative.

It didn't worry me terribly, and I thought the combination of Greer and Hancock a very good one.

*

The show brought me one great stroke of good fortune, the chance to work with a man with whom I became good friends, the director Vernon Lawrence.

His father, Douglas Lawrence, had been a BBC radio producer, and Vernon, although destined for the Church, found that prospect irksome and opted for the BBC where he started in radio as a sound-effects boy. Later he crossed to television as ASM, then Floor Manager, and then Director.

In the years that have followed I've worked with Vernon on quite a few occasions and have seen him grow in stature from junior director to Head of Light Entertainment at Yorkshire Television, where his assurance, skill and ability to deal with people make him an outstanding figure in an industry in which there are all too few people of his calibre.

Our next job together was a pilot programme for a new series to be called *Grubstreet*, adaptations of the work of various Fleet Street humorists including Nat Gubbins, J.B. Morton, Alan

Coren and the *Private Eye* team; and Michael Green, whose contribution to the Peter Simple column in the *Daily Telegraph* – the adventures of the eighteenth-century rake, Squire Haggard – I found hilarious.

*

I had strayed into the world of journalism the previous year with an article for *Punch* about the Royal Command Performance.

In the late sixties and early seventies there was hardly anyone of any calibre in the field of humorous writing and drawing who didn't at one time or another write for *Punch*, and I was fairly apprehensive when I submitted my first article. But the commission for a second and then a third soon came in, and before long I became a regular contributor, either with ad hoc articles or with book reviews or, when the main line critics went on holiday, writing film and theatre criticism.

The best part of writing for *Punch* was being invited to their weekly lunches. These took place on Wednesday, by which time all the copy for that week's edition was in.

Apart from the regulars there was always one or more guests at the table, generally politicians or royalty.

Prince Philip, polite and urbane, appeared to eat rather a lot of butter but otherwise was a perfect guest. The politicians of whatever party often tried to use it as a platform for some party rhetoric, but this was quickly if politely squashed by the assembled hacks and cartoonists. I can remember Margaret Thatcher holding forth on the virtues of Winston Churchill as the bringer of social reforms back in 1912. Someone drily commented, 'Ah, but he was a Liberal then.' The Liberal leader, Jeremy Thorpe who, I felt, looked more like a bookie than a potential prime minister, gave marvellous imitations of his foes and colleagues. Vic Feather, the Trade Union leader, sparkled, Willie Whitelaw was wildly indiscreet, and various other folk from show business and literature chatted amiably, lucidly or amusingly, while the older members of the *Punch* table dozed over their port.

In the seventies the Editor, Bill Davis, though often absent, was never out of touch and was very keen on special events.

Alan Coren, the deputy Editor, when in charge kept this idea of special occasions firmly in mind and between them they produced some brilliant, readable, original editions of the magazine – no mean feat for an organ that had been wheezing away since 1841. Since 1971 things have changed radically, and when Alan Coren departed after ten years as Editor, having replaced Bill Davis in 1978, there was a rapid deterioration; and today, on the rare occasions I've looked at the magazine, I must admit to being shocked and dismayed by the tatty and unfunny mess it has become. Perhaps I'm just getting old and don't get the point any more; but looking back, in the seventies it was not only sharp and funny but well-written and beautifully produced with covers (the best by Trog or Geoffrey Dickinson) of often outstanding design and style.

Coming from radio and television I found writing for print difficult at first, and once I'd run out of autobiographical pieces (Alan Coren enjoyed my reminiscences of my music hall days) I found writing *humour* impossible.

Being a critic, however, whether of books, plays, films or tv, is no problem. After all, someone else has done the work, all you have to do is comment on it.

One thing a critic must strive for, even if it means gritting his teeth and battling against the tide of other people's opinions, is honest appraisal. Insight, the gift of the great critics, is not given to many, and only rarely to the best. It is a very warm feeling to spot a star or see a film maker's intentions clearly, or observe something that others have missed, but that is a rare treat and is to be savoured and treasured when it occurs.

I learned when I became one myself, that no professional critic wants any show he reviews to be anything but a success.

The reason so many plays and musicals get panned is that they disappoint and don't live up to the critics' expectations, which are often fuelled by optimistic advance publicity or over-eager Public Relations people.

You can't fake a hit, and though many shows that I have thought mediocre have had a long run and others which I've felt are excellent have closed all too soon, the groundswell of public opinion generally sorts out the good and popular from the dull or pretentious. Of course fashion plays a part, and the name of Tom

Stoppard or Alan Ayckbourn will fill any theatre for a time. If you add the name of John Gielgud or Felicity Kendal full-theatre time will lengthen, and with both Sir John and Felicity Kendal in a musical with the book by Harold Pinter and music by Andrew Lloyd Webber the damn thing would probably run forever.

But the mathematics of the theatre are different from other areas of show business. A tv play that attracts only a million viewers is thought to be a flop. If a million people saw that same play at, say, the Apollo Theatre in Shaftesbury Avenue it would run for over a thousand performances and make everybody concerned a great deal of money.

A critic goes to the theatre aware that what he says about the play may influence a married couple to spend a lot of money on an evening out, and if they don't like the play their wrath will be directed at the critic. I suppose a long stint of reviewing first nights (and there's always a cry of 'foul' from the management if the critic goes to a preview) might deaden the appetite, but on the whole live theatre is an exciting experience and even at its worst at least it's there, happening at the time you see it.

With films it's different. A movie could have been made up to three or four years before you get to see it, and thousands of miles away. All but the best somehow lose their flavour on their journey to the preview theatre, and watching up to four films a day, as a film critic might reasonably be expected to do, leaves you with an appetite jaded by repetition.

*

Towards the end of my time as the principal film critic of *Punch*, so promoted by Bill Davis and carrying on under Alan Coren, I became sickened by the ghastly ritual of 10 am Wardour Street previews, and sandwiches and white wine hand-outs by mediocre film companies.

When Alan Coren became Editor I promised him a year of undivided loyalty as film critic, but when that year was up I was replaced by the octogenarian Dilys Powell, recently retired from the *Sunday Times*, who was born before the movies existed and was still reviewing them long after they had shown any sign of life. She, more than anybody, understood the cinema and was more fitted than I to record the weekly hits and misses of the silver screen.

*

During the time I was the *Punch* film critic my almost constant companion at the screenings was Michael ffolkes, the cartoonist, who drew a picture each week to accompany my column. At his best he was a fine artist, imaginative and skilful, but he was also a heavy drinker and womaniser and was often under par.

He persuaded me, against my better judgment, to write a comic strip with him, which we never sold, and later to collaborate on a play, called *French Lessons*, which was set in a West End flat that had once been a brothel but was now an artist's studio (ffolkes's main contribution would have been to supply the paintings). It was, of course, a farce with the central part, the artist's valet, written with Kenneth Williams in mind. It was frankly awful and quite rightly turned down by Michael Codron, the impresario. I never offered it to anyone else, as it's a shaming process to have one's work rejected and you have to be thick-skinned, or fairly conceited, not to accept the first refusal as final.

On the whole I get on with cartoonists who, like comedy writers, are a breed haunted by doubt and only placated by cash, booze or broads, and while I admire a number of them, to me and many others, today's outstanding political cartoonist and caricaturist is the *Observer*'s award-winning Wally Fawkes, otherwise known as Trog. Wally and I met at *Punch* at one of the Wednesday lunches and formed a friendship based on mutual admiration. I was enormously flattered when some time later he asked me to work with him on the *Daily Mail* cartoon strip, Flook.

Previous writers of the strip, which had run for years, had included Compton Mackenzie, Humphrey Lyttleton and, best of all, George Melly. When Melly felt he'd had enough, Barry Norman took over and when he departed Wally Fawkes asked me.

Our routine was to meet at Wally's home in north-west London and discuss, over several glasses of white wine, indeed on occasions several bottles of white wine, a possible story line. On the whole these stories ran, on a six-day-a-week basis, for three months and were loosely based on contemporary themes and people. I would write a week at a time, deliver the bubbles on Monday, discuss what would follow, and go home to write it.

Flook, a small, furry intellectual with various magic powers, and the boy Rufus, had a number of adventures involving a Private Army in the Home Counties, Invisible Exports, Concorde, a spy in 10 Downing Street and, most successfully and totally Wally's idea, a story based on the Peasants' Revolt, with Rufus as King Richard II the boy king, Flook as Friar Flook his tutor, while the various historical goodies and baddies were depicted as seventies politicians: Michael Foot, Tony Benn, Margaret Thatcher, Ted Heath, Enoch Powell and so forth.

After two years working on the strip I felt I couldn't continue, and although I think he was hurt, Wally accepted it. He'd been particularly generous to me, even giving me a 'script by' by-line, the first time a writer had been credited since Compton Mackenzie many years before. Our friendship endured, but although when Wally left the *Daily Mail* and Flook was taken on by Robert Maxwell for the *Daily Mirror* I was asked to work on the strip again, I felt that Flook was part of my past and should stay that way.

15

The Grim Reaper – deferred

In August 1973 I was approached to put together a book of *Round the Horne* scripts for the publishers Woburn Press. Woburn had been successful with their books of *Goon Show* scripts and had also published *The Best of Morecambe and Wise, Till Death Us Do Part* scripts, *Hancock's Half Hour* and *ITMA* and wanted to add *Round the Horne* to their list. I assembled the book, which was illustrated by William Hewison, the Art Editor of *Punch*, wrote a foreword and a glossary of the terms used by Julian and Sandy, and added a clutch of Rambling Syd Rumpo songs. It looked good and sold well.

The routine of life, a little television, some journalism and regular radio appearances continued fairly smoothly into 1974. In May, after producing the pilot for a satirical series called *The BBC Regrets* (which was never made), I went into the London Clinic for a check-up.

I'd been having some trouble with my urine – sometimes it was like peeing rusty fragments of corrugated iron – and it was felt that an examination was in order.

I was duly installed in a room the London Clinic, ate a good dinner, and worked on my current piece for *Punch*, an article about the emerging snobbery in some quarters over mineral water. For instance, the oneupmanship of ordering Badoit rather than Perrier and the rival virtues of the still waters available. In the mid-seventies bottled water was just becoming fashionable in the UK and the brewers and other interested parties had woken up to the fact that there was money to be made with the stuff. Bill Davis had spotted this and commissioned me to write a tongue-in-cheek essay on the subject. I actually finished the article five minutes before the nurse came in to give me my pre-med injection. I was duly wheeled up to the operating theatre where surgeon Mr Howard Hanley and anaesthetist Dr Brian Day were waiting.

I was put to sleep and woke up some hours later with tubes seemingly coming out of every orifice, including one I hadn't had that morning. It transpired that I had cancer of the bladder. A large tumour had been removed and here I was strung up like a Christmas decoration, feeling decidedly off colour.

The days went by and I gradually felt more myself and could even consider chatting up the nurses, who were a cheery bunch and whom, naturally enough, I came to know quite well.

One morning a couple of them came into my room giggling over a cartoon in a newspaper. It was of a man almost entirely swathed in bandages being taken for a dip in the sea, helped by two nurses. 'Look,' my two said, 'he looks just like you', and shrieked with laughter. As luck would have it, the cartoon was by my friend Stan McMurtry, MAC of the *Daily Mail*. Later that day I asked Lyn to ask Stan if I could buy the original to give to the nurses. He of course gave me the original and even added a Took reference. The nurses were suitably impressed.

The night sister, who had looked after me for what was apparently a worrying time immediately after the operation, was much in the mould of the dedicated profession she adorned. Her name was Vicki, and after I came out of hospital we met once or twice in order for me to thank her. Dimly, through a fog of pain-killing drugs, I remember this caring, attentive person and when quite recently (in 1989) she turned up in the audience of a *News Quiz* recording and came over afterwards to say hello, I was again overwhelmed by feelings of gratitude for her care and concern.

Lyn was with me night and day, of course, and always there when I wanted her.

*

When you're in hospital for any length of time you become acutely aware of other people's attitudes and behaviour, especially visitors. Kenny Everett at that time had an early morning radio show on Capital Radio and he would send me greetings over the air, and informed his listeners one morning, re me, 'He's had it all taken away. He's no more than an eyeball on a stick', which made me laugh so much it hurt.

Further changes in the admin of the BBC TV Light Entertainment department saw James Gilbert as Head of Comedy, replacing Duncan Wood who had gone to Yorkshire Television as their Head of Light Entertainment. He visited me and brought me comic books to cheer me up. Bill Cotton didn't visit but phoned and spent ten minutes telling me of his impending holiday in the West Indies, and going on at great length about how he hated flying. At that time I was looking forward to being allowed out of bed and the thought of walking to the bathroom unaided was my greatest ambition.

Two friends, John Goldstone and Jim Clark, came more than once: Jim cheerful and chatty, full of gossip and good will, John more restrained but welcome. He turned up on his own one evening and prowled round the room, obviously troubled by something. I asked him what was the matter. He said that he had the chance to produce the first original Monty Python film, *Monty Python and the Holy Grail* and did I think it was a good idea. I assured him it was. What was the budget? £143,000 he told me. I said, 'Christ, John, you'll get that back in the UK. The rest of the world will be all profit.' He cheered up a bit at that, but then became gloomy again when he told me that the film would be directed by Terry Jones *and* Terry Gilliam. Two directors – could this lead to trouble? I said that, provided he, John, had the final say in the editing of the film, he was safe.

Thus heartened, he decided to go ahead. It was a wise move as the film (and for my money it was the best of all the Python pictures) made an enormous profit and led the way to more success for the Python team worldwide.

John Goldstone and Jim Clark, incidentally, had become friends of mine some years before, as respectively a young assistant producer and film editor to producer Joseph Janni, they came to Marty and me with the suggestion that we write a film for Kenneth Williams. Why we didn't I don't know, but as a result of that first meeting John, Jim and I became close friends. As the years have gone on so their careers in films have grown success by success, with Jim reaching a peak in 1987 when he won the Oscar for his work in editing *Killing Fields*.

John has a become a highly successful film producer with movies like *Monty Python's Life of Brian, The Rocky Horror Picture Show* and *Eric the Viking* to his credit.

Back in '74 John and Jim still had some way to go but oozed talent and were engaging and amusing companions.

Alan Coren came to see me regularly while I was in hospital and was unflaggingly helpful to Lyn, even offering to baby-sit while she visited me.

Elinor, who was six, came to see me when I was on the mend, and later on at a school open day I was slightly astonished to see pinned to the classroom wall her drawing of me in the hospital bed complete with catheter and the rest of the paraphernalia of a bladder operation. My discomfort was no secret to Class 2 of Robinsfield Primary School.

I recovered fairly quickly and came home, and after a period of recuperation we went on a motoring holiday to Normandy and Brittany. Frankie Howerd, who had visited me more than once in hospital, offered to lend us his house in Malta, but I didn't fancy the long air journey, particularly as I was instructed by Mr Hanley, the surgeon, to drink a minimum of ten pints of liquid a day. Driving through France I could stop by the road side whenever I wished, but the thought of constantly visiting the lavatory on a crowded aircraft didn't appeal to me at all.

Being of an impulsive disposition I insisted on bathing in the sea once we reached St Aubin in Normandy. Our hotel resembled the one in *M. Hulot's Holiday*, and the little resort and plage were modestly cheerful. It was early July and the sea was much colder than I'd expected.

I nearly froze and was duly revived by an extremely hot bath. For the rest of that holiday I was more cautious and it passed without further incident.

*

Back home I started a long series of *The Impressionists* on Radio 2, a series featuring mimics and impersonators – not, as some listeners at first supposed, a discussion of nineteenth-century

French painting – and I started making regular appearances in Radio Four's Arts programme, *Kaleidoscope*. I still do the occasional piece of instant criticism of theatre or tv for the programme, which is an important part of the BBC's radio output, and it's an honour to be part of it. The trouble is that what you're asked to review often isn't as good as the programme you're reviewing it on. I remember one play, a fairly threadbare farce starring Brian Rix and Jimmy Logan called *A Bit Between the Teeth*, of which I said, 'We've had the Theatre of Cruelty and the Theatre of the Absurd, what we have here is apparently the Theatre of the Deaf as members of the cast walk down to the footlights and shout the plot at the audience.'

The most important, and certainly the most enjoyable, radio programme I was involved with in 1974 was *Who Are You Arthur Marshall?* It was an idea I'd had some time before which combined a sort of lighthearted *Face to Face* set up, a one-to-one interview with interesting people – hence the who-are-you of the title – plus the use of a *small* audience of no more than twenty people, friends and relatives of the person the programme was about. I'd grown bored by the braying studio audiences of those days and wanted chuckles and reflective smiles: chamber music as opposed to Mahler symphonies.

Arthur Marshall, whom I'd met when he was a guest on *Sounds Familiar*, seemed an ideal subject, especially as I'd cut my comic teeth on impersonations of Arthur, who was a regular radio performer pre-war and whose female impersonations I had loved. I was also besotted with his journalism, for as a book critic he had no equal, and his humour column in the *New Statesman* and subsequently the *Sunday Telegraph* was required reading.

So a small audience was assembled and Arthur and I chatted about his life. He resurrected his characterisation of Nurse Dugdale, and read snatches of his girls' school stories written in the manner of Angela Brazil, and a thoroughly good time was had by all.

The programme went out in mid-afternoon some time later, but the idea was never taken up by the BBC as it fell rather awkwardly between the two stools of the Talks department and Light Entertainment.

In television things were a little brighter. My producer's

contract had not been renewed because after my hospitalisation it was thought, by me as well as the BBC, that I couldn't effectively or efficiently work a normal nine-to-five day. I found out later that various people in the Light Entertainment department had got hold of the notion that my condition was terminal and that if I snuffed it while under contract the BBC would have to pay Lyn a widow's pension.

However, James Gilbert, with great generosity, offered me the option of writing anything I wished. I suggested two or three ideas and the one he preferred was an adaptation of Stephen Potter's books, *Oneupmanship, Gamesmanship* and *Lifemanship*.

Bernard Thompson was deputed to produce it, and Bernard, who had been James Gilbert's floor manager on a number of successful series and had been promoted on James's elevation, seemed a good idea. His choice to play the leading role was Richard Briers, who was excellent, and the supporting team of Peter Jones and Freddie Jaeger couldn't have been bettered.

As was usual we started with a pilot programme, a special Christmas edition. It was well received and a series duly scheduled.

*

I was still having to make regular hospital visits and all was not well with my poor old bladder. The ten-pints-a-day ritual designed to expand the bladder back to its pre-operation size – the op had reduced the surface area of the bladder considerably – had worked and the pain and discomfort of passing water had abated, but unwelcome things were still growing and Howard Hanley was battling to save the organ. Had things got worse it would have meant another major op to remove bladder and other encumbrances and replace them with tube and bag.

Now I know that having that inconvenience wouldn't have been the end of the world, but I would certainly be better off without that drastic step having to be taken. In an attempt to halt the growth of whatever it was in my bladder I was given a course of radiotherapy as an outpatient at the Royal Free Hospital at Hampstead. There I was examined, measured and calibrated, and the exact area to receive the X-rays was pinpointed. Then for five days a week I'd be strapped to the slab and rotated to the exact position required. Nurse and operator would scamper out of the room, the heavy lead-faced door would be closed and I'd be alone with my fate. It didn't take long and it didn't hurt, and apart from considerable bowel disorders and defoliation of my pubic hair I didn't suffer much in the way of after-effects.

After two trips to the London Clinic, whose clients came mostly from the Middle East, Howard Hanley thought it would be better for me to go to the King Edward VII Hospital for Officers in Beaumont Street, where he was a consultant.

The snag was I hadn't been an officer, but somehow I was allowed in. Howard Hanley was so senior and so respected that I think his word was enough. I did prefer it and got to know nurses, sisters and matrons well over the years that followed. Once I'd become a regular it was taken as read that if my family needed treatment they would naturally go to 'Sister Aggie's', as the King Edward VII was affectionately known, Sister Agnes Keyser having founded it in 1899.

In 1976 I was going in for a check cystoscopy every three months, and in July came the crunch when Howard Hanley would make the fatal decision whether or not to perform the major op.

I was prepared for the main event with a series of embarrassing routines, enemas, shaving, etc., and before he went to scrub up Howard came to see me. I said to him that I was prepared for any eventuality but that if he could spare me I'd be grateful. He said he'd do his best, and the ritual of pre-med and the journey on the hospital trolley to the operating theatre duly commenced. Brian Day, the anaesthetist, had the endearing habit of telling slightly salacious, allegedly true stories as he put you to sleep. One was to the effect that from the recovery room window he had been able to see Christine Keeler and her callers who were ... I never found out who because he'd timed things so precisely that I was out for the count before he needed to elaborate.

One of his other stories concerned the Arab at the London Clinic. It seems that this poor chap, a highly regarded servant of a megarich sheik, developed some eye trouble and the sheik sent him to London for treatment. The Arab arrived, was put in a private room and told to relax, the doctor would be in to see him in ten minutes. With ten minutes to kill the Arab wandered out into the corridor – after all this was his first time in England and he was curious. He saw a pair of handsome double doors, slightly ajar, with polished handles and with a notice hanging from one of them. Not speaking English he didn't read the notice but, opening the doors, walked through and fell down the lift shaft. The notice had read 'Lift Out Of Order. Do Not Touch These Doors'. So the Arab was found at the bottom of the lift shaft with a broken collar bone, a broken leg and three fractured ribs. He couldn't explain what had happened or what room he was in before the accident.

The entire hospital was searched until the unfortunate Arab and his room were united. His injuries were, of course, treated instantly and with great care, the workman who'd left the lift doors open was reprimanded, and from then on every patient at the hospital had a wristband affixed the moment he or she arrived.

Now, I don't believe a word of it either, but it was Dr Day's special brand of amusing anecdotes that made him such an excellent anaesthetist, sending his patients off into dreamland with a smile. Both Dr Day and Mr Hanley became friends, and as you can imagine my gratitude for their brilliant skills and helpful manner is unbounded.

As it turned out, the X-ray treatment had done its work and I didn't need that major operation, and in September 1975 Howard Hanley wrote to me, 'I am delighted with your progress.' Today my visits to hospital for check-ups are annual. Mr Hanley and Dr Day have retired and several other surgeons have looked after me since then.

To date, and I touch wood as I write this, there has been no recurrence of my bladder disorder, and smoking, which indirectly was the cause, is no longer one of my vices, as I stopped smoking in 1982.

When your health goes you really appreciate the medical profession, their skill and dedication. I was lucky that I could afford to have private treatment, but it seems disgraceful that the finest medical care is not immediately available for everyone who needs it irrespective of income.

Doctors, surgeons and nurses do their best, but it must be like fighting a forest fire with an eggcupful of water to keep our NHS hospitals and clinics running efficiently.

In the private sector, on the other hand, skill, efficiency and speed go hand in hand and the results are first-class.

The King Edward VII Hospital is typical of these strengths in British medicine even though the facilities are not of the finest – well, certainly not in comparison with the London Clinic, the Wellington, the Humana and half a dozen others of which I have experience. Where King Edward VII scores is in prestige (Royalty and senior politicians are regular visitors) and atmosphere. Where it falls down is in a shortage of bathrooms. Very few rooms have a bathroom en suite, a situation which could have led to acute embarrassment on one occasion.

Lyn had been having gynaecological problems and was operated on first for a cyst and then two years later, to the regret of Mr (now Sir) George Pinker who was looking after her, a hysterectomy. Both ops were completely successful and after the latter and two weeks of recuperation, Lyn was given the glad tidings that she could go home the following day. She was in one of the coveted rooms with bath, and Matron approached her with a request. Would Lyn please vacate the room and spend her last night in the hospital in a smaller, less well equipped room. The Duchess of – well, for the sake of discretion let's say a duchess – was coming into the hospital later that day and they would like to give her the better room. Lyn gladly agreed, moved, and then phoned me to inform me of the change of location.

Come visiting time I turned up, and out of curiosity peered through the small window set in the door of my wife's erstwhile room. There was the duchess fast asleep in bed, her long blonde hair spread across the pillow. I tiptoed away but then the imp of mischief that has been my undoing on more than one occasion seized me and I went, poker-faced, into Sister's room and said: 'Look, it's a bit thick. I went into my wife's room and in order to cheer her up I said, "Hey, darling, it's your loving husband. You'll be in your own bed tomorrow and then wha hey!!" But then I saw this strange blonde woman in the bed. It was really quite embarrassing.'

Sister went white, took me to Lyn's new room and then sped away. Two minutes later the deputy Matron appeared, out of breath, full of apologies that I hadn't been told. Shortly after, Matron herself came and made a similar apology. I explained that it was a joke and no protocol had been breached, but I think the nursing staff were too much in a state of shock to do anything but shudder at the prospect of the duchess being so disturbed.

When we told the story to Howard Hanley and Brian Day when later they strolled in to pay Lyn a social visit, they roared with laughter and I have a sneaking feeling that Dr Day added the story to the catalogue of improbable and improper tales he told to relax his patients.

*

By the end of 1974 I was writing regularly for *Punch*, involved in the daily Flook strip cartoon, planning *Oneupmanship*, chairing *The Impressionists*, had put up the idea of a tv revue based on *Punch* and had started work on a history of radio comedy called *Laughter in the Air*. But something more important and more intriguing than any other projects had been offered and I looked forward to 1975 with eagerness at the prospect of, to quote *Monty Python's Flying Circus* – 'something completely different'.

16

On the Move

I suppose that if I had to name the three show business ventures I've most enjoyed being involved with they would be *Points of View, Round the Horne* and *On the Move*, the 1970s BBC Literacy Project. In 1975, while I was still visiting hospital regularly, I had a phone call from one David Hargreaves, a producer in the BBC TV Further Education Department (now known as Continuing Education). He'd heard that I'd written two books of plays (published by Cassells) for children with reading difficulties, and he was planning a tv project designed to help adults who had somehow slipped through the education net and could neither read nor write. Would I be interested in contributing? I was, and David Hargreaves and the director of the projected series, Barbara Derkow, came to see me.

They outlined the problem: an estimated three million British adults had considerable difficulty with reading and writing and in many cases had no literacy skills at all.

The three million figure did not include ethnic minorities or children, and frankly I was staggered at the size of the problem. Many years before I had been astounded, when in the RAF, to find that two Scottish ex-miners had signed on so that they could be taught to read and write and learn a trade, but I had assumed that apart from these men who felt inadequate and wanted literally to get out of the pit, and the ineducable minority, illiteracy was a minor problem.

Apparently the problem was approaching crisis proportions, and in co-operation with the ILEA (Inner London Education Authority), the Ford Foundation, the Cadbury Trust, the Tesco grocery chain and other interested parties who supplied facilities, publicity and money, the BBC was planning a long-running weekly series of programmes to help people conquer their fear of words and their shame at being illiterate, and promote an atmosphere where they would attend classes in their home locality and, as it were, come out of the illiterate closet.

David Hargreaves told me that plans were well advanced, that scripts were being written by, among others, Fay Weldon, and that a starry cast including Patricia Hayes, Polly James, Rosemary Leach, Norman Rossington, Nigel Stock, Martin Shaw and Gay Hamilton had been assembled. There was to be a science fiction sketch where on some planet on a far-off galaxy the illiterate were treated as slaves. I seem to remember it had a sort of Spartacus theme. Then there was a miniature soap opera cum domestic series in which a visitor from another planet lived with a working-class family and, of course, had to have explained what things were, and have the names of various objects written down.

There were also two animators, Ted Rockley and Derek Phillips, working on Disneyfying various letters of the alphabet and simple words – brilliantly as it turned out, and almost the best things in the eventual series. I was to provide a lighter note, a touch of humour, a chuckle or two to lighten the teaching load.

The idea I came up with for the pilot programme was a letter shop in which, rather like a furniture store, the would-be purchaser could consider various letters in a variety of styles to suit his or her taste. Peter Jones played the salesman, gaily offering 'a nice set of occasional w's', or 'three-piece c's'. It was all very frothy and light, as it was meant to be, and the idea behind it was that letters (and thus literacy) were as useful as chairs and tables.

A pilot was duly made containing all these ingredients, and to get the reactions of a sample of the people the project was aimed at, David Hargreaves and Barbara Derkow showed the film to a selected group of inmates at Wormwood Scrubs Prison.

To get the full picture you must realise that David Hargreaves was of slight build, wore spectacles and was earnest and intellectual; Barbara Derkow was more hearty but just as intellectual; and, more important, both were (and still are) idealists, and experienced teachers of foreign languages.

Enter something in the region of a hundred inmates of 'the Scrubs' serving various terms of imprisonment for such crimes as assault with a deadly weapon, armed robbery and grievous bodily harm.

David speaks: 'Now, I know this is not usual but the governor has given you leave to say exactly what you think about the film we are going to show you. You probably won't like it all, but we'd like your honest opinion.'

Then they showed the prisoners the film and waited for reactions. I think that the violence of the reaction shattered David and Barbara, because when they returned to the Television Centre and we asked them eagerly how things had gone they were white-faced and, for a while, speechless. Eventually they choked out what had been said. Leaving out the expletives, some of which I suspect they had only ever seen written down in 'progressive' novels – it didn't amount to much.

The reaction of the inmates of Wormwood Scrubs to the Adult Literacy Project was, in short, that it was a load of patronising, middle-class rubbish. This was something of a setback as the whole thrust of the idea had been to get away from the 'BBC teaches the Bourgeoisie' manner of some earlier educational programmes.

Clearly none of the sketches had worked. The soap looked and sounded stupid, the science fiction was incomprehensible, and the letter shop was a disaster. So, back to the drawing-board … but, alas, the drawing-board stayed resolutely blank.

Then I had an idea. Why not have a pair of characters who, like a Greek chorus, could comment on the action? To react as the convicted criminals had. David and Barbara leapt at the suggestion, and after a long and creative session we came up with the following scenario.

Alf and Bert (A and B, geddit!) are lorry driver and mate, one illiterate, the other not. They are furniture removers (that gives them access to many different environments. E.g. imagine them packing the books from a library and Bert, the illiterate, wondering what is the point of all that print if the owner couldn't have read it all in his lifetime.)

Let's make Bert a sharp, streetwise cockney, and his mate, Alf, a soft, mild, literate north-countryman. Let Bert be taking the BBC Literacy Course, and having difficulties and complaining about its middle-class leanings ... and so on. Ah, but who was to play these key roles?

I'd seen Bob Hoskins in a play called *Veterans*, starring John Gielgud and John Mills, in which Bob played a film technician on location. I thought he was wonderful and David Hargreaves, who had also seen and been impressed by Bob, agreed. For his friend and companion (the only person in whom the Hoskins character confided his illiteracy and his struggle to learn to read and write) David suggested Donald Gee. It was a wonderful choice, as Donald selflessly and calmly helped the whole enterprise to succeed.

I wrote half a dozen short scripts to see if the idea worked in practice, it did and we were back in business.

The only things to survive from the pilot were the animation sequences and, of course, the simple word-recognition films emphasising how important words like Push and Pull, Open and Closed, In and Out, On and Off were in everyone's everyday life.

David Hargreaves, in a fit of optimism, had given all the actors long contracts, but as everything they had been contracted to do had been scrapped there was a major problem. I was asked, shyly, would I write a number of sketches for them that would be neither patronising or obscure.

The short answer is that I did. The actors gave some stunning performances, Gee and Hoskins being outstanding as Alf and Bert. We made fifty ten-minute programmes, each of which was repeated nine times, and Dennis Potter, who was tv critic of the *New Statesman* at the time, had this to say in the issue of 7 November 1975:

> On the Move: a series of short programmes using all the resources and power of the medium to educate some of its audience, and help to lift them from the chains of ignorance and shame. It works marvellously well ... Indeed I think it must be just about the most succinct, elegant and inspiring series now running on tv partly because of the zest of the wittily animated graphics, and the gaiety of the minuscule dramas, but mostly for the total lack of condescension or shiftiness of purpose which so often characterises tv programmes not slotted into the huge 'entertainment holes'.

The cast booked originally for those failed serials were asked if they'd stay on in the revised version of the show, and all but one agreed.

To be honest, I really enjoyed writing for these glittering performers, inventing sketches which illustrated words or groups of letters (e.g. double O as in book, look, cook etc.) which they performed like mini-dramas and which were, because of the acting skill and Barbara Derkow's neat and unfussy direction, extremely effective. There's no doubt, however, that Bob Hoskins and Donald Gee were the stars of the show and in the one hundred plus short scenes I wrote for them they were able to convey the agony and shame, the anger, frustration and finally the victory of tackling illiteracy.

The series attracted an audience of millions and I'm sure that one of the reasons for its success was the fact that it was not *obviously* for the illiterate. It could be, and was, watched by young and old, literate and illiterate alike, for its entertainment value.

At the end of each programme one of the cast would appeal to the non-readers and -writers in the viewing audience to phone a number for details of where they could get help in their own locality. After every programme the phone lines were jammed and many people found their way to classes or individual tutors and learned for themselves the value of being literate.

The feedback from the people who wanted to learn was remarkable. One man, when asked why he wanted to read, came up with the surprising answer that he was sick of going on holiday to Whitstable. Not that he had anything against the place but, living in the Midlands, it was the only resort to which he'd memorised the route, road signs being meaningless to him. He wanted to be able to read signposts and maps so that he could bring a bit of variety into his vacations.

Another case was of two young men who arrived at the ILEA literacy centre and asked for details of the course. It turned out they were members of the National Front but couldn't read the literature.

That opened the argument as to whether it was better to educate people than to leave them in 'blissful' ignorance. The answer was, of course, that although a little knowledge might be a dangerous thing, no knowledge at all can be fatal.

Still, it was surprising to discover that many people with quite important jobs in industry had managed to hide their lack of learning for many years.

Illiterates are, by and large, not stupid, and in many cases their illiteracy stems from two sources. One: they are from homes where there is no literature of any kind, not even a tabloid newspaper. Two: the parent doesn't want the child to leave home and illiteracy means dependence on the parent. Some children unconsciously refuse to learn so as not to leave Mum. After all, how do you cope with the outside world if you can't read or write?

Many literate people don't read much. I recently met a very likeable, well-educated, middle-class woman who confessed that she didn't read at all in England but enjoyed the novels of Jeffrey Archer when she was on holiday! But it does seem inconceivable that a normal, healthy adult can go through life without being able to decipher the many printed signs that are all around. Although *On the Move* helped over one hundred thousand people to read (and the effect that must have had, not only on the student but on his or her friends and relatives, must have been considerable), its main effect was to remove the fear and shame of illiteracy. It was no longer a taboo subject, and what's more it produced a star.

Dennis Potter's next venture into series writing was *Pennies from Heaven*, and the lead was played by the man who had so impressed him in *On the Move*, Bob Hoskins.

The following year it was decided to change the format, and *Your Move*, as this second stage of the project was called, consisted of twenty-six half-hour programmes fronted by Brian Redhead, and was a much more formal approach to education. My task was to provide a sketch for each programme, illustrating how, one by one, each letter of the alphabet was used in everday situations. Well, I say 'everyday', but I was able to get away with some pretty way-out solutions to the problems.

What helped was the fact that every major television personality who was approached agreed to take part and our cast list for the series included almost every popular performer of the day – John Alderton and Pauline Collins, Arthur Lowe,

Ian Lavender, Fulton McKay, Frederick Jaeger, Julia McKenzie, Andrew Sachs, Millicent Martin, Frank Thornton, Tim Brooke-Taylor, Thora Hird, Denis Waterman, Robert Morley, Joan Sims, Brian Wilde, Wilfred Brambell, Michael Gambon, Eric Sykes, Robin Bailey, Terence Alexander, Dandy Nichols and many more.

In programme 20 of the series the letter to be promoted was L. I was stumped for a bit but then came up with the following.

The premise is that the Sistine Chapel has just been completed. The papal nuncio, Cardinal Bramante of Urbino, was played by Brian Wilde (very much in the character he used as Warder Barraclough in *Porridge*, a dithering north-countryman). Michaelangelo was played by Ray Brooks as a chirpy 'with it' cockney. (NB The words beginning with L are introduced fairly naturally and without comment by the actors. Brian Redhead, in his introduction, warned the audience to be on the look out for the frequency and variety of the use of the letter L.)

Fade up:
Part of the Sistine Chapel in the year 1508. It is, as yet, undecorated.
Enter Bramante of Urbino and Michaelangelo.
They look up at ceiling.

BRAMANTE:	Well, this is it, Michaelangelo, the Sistine Chapel.
MICHAELANGELO:	Bit on the large side, isn't it? ... Not to say lofty. It's not so much the breadth as the length – that's going to be the trouble.
BRAMANTE:	Well, yes, it is, but his Holiness thought it'd be something to get your teeth into.
MICHAELANGELO:	It means laying on my back to do that ceiling – not to mention up and down ladders all day mixing paint.
BRAMANTE:	Well?
MICHAELANGELO:	My lumbago's giving me gyp, and it's not a ten-minute job, is it? It's going to be four and a half years if its a day.
BRAMANTE:	As long as that?
MICHAELANGELO:	Yes. Mind you, I can't start till Tuesday.
BRAMANTE:	But it's wanted for Lent. Can't you get a lad in to give you a hand? I've heard that Leonardo da Vinci is quite good.
MICHAELANGELO:	What, Len? Well, if you want a ceiling full of

cartoons he's your man, but he's hopeless on ceilings. By the way, what *do* you fancy up there?

BRAMANTE: I don't know. We thought you could advise us.

MICHAELANGELO: Well, fruit's nice. You could have a vast bowl of fruit – apples, oranges, lemons, lychees, loganberries, limes, a few grapes. I done one like that for a fruiterer up Livorno.

BRAMANTE: No, I don't think ... for a chapel ... we were really hoping for something more biblical.

MICHAELANGELO: What about fish? They're biblical. You could have Moses and Abraham over there sharing a bowl of jellied eels, and over there you could have Solomon in all his glory tucking into a lobster. Yes, I like that. Nice splash of colour a lobster. Then I could do you a few frescoes of crabs and limpets.

Bramante shakes his head.

MICHAELANGELO: Flowers? A nice flower scene? Lupins, lilies, long-stemmed roses, and those little blue ones – what are they called?

BRAMANTE: Forget-me-nots.

MICHAELANGELO: That's them. Well, what do you think?

Bramante shrugs.

MICHAELANGELO: Look – how much you reckoning to pay for all this?

BRAMANTE: Well, I'm afraid the treasurer said not a penny over three hundred lire an hour, plus materials.

MICHAELANGELO: That all?

BRAMANTE: I'm afraid so.

MICHAELANGELO: I'll tell you what you'll get for that, my old son –

BRAMANTE: What?

MICHAELANGELO: Two coats of white emulsion.

As the series advanced, people starting saying to me, 'Ah, the letters L and M and O are easy to illustrate, but what about Z?' In fact that was the easiest. I wrote a parody of the popular American tv series *The Mark of Zorro*, with Andrew Sachs as the incompetent hero and Millicent Martin whom he is seeking to rescue. It turns out he's in the wrong hacienda and the damsel in distress lives up the road.

David Hargreaves produced, but directing chores were shared between Barbara Derkow, Caroline Pick and Doug Willcox. I didn't feel the same involvement with *Your Move* as I had with *On the Move*, and in fact I don't think it was nearly as effective. The third year of the project consisted of thirteen programmes called *Write Away* which was designed to help people improve their handwriting. I was asked to front the programme and this, somewhat reluctantly, I did.

The series was produced jointly by Caroline Pick and Jonathan Stenhouse and the whole project was a triumph of common sense and reason over those in the BBC who felt that it was venturing into territory it would have been better to avoid.

I can remember in the early days, before the programmes had gone out, Huw Wheldon, then Managing Director, Television, calling a cheery warning to me as he strode across the entrance hall of the TV Centre, 'Remember, don't be didactic, Took.' My reply was 'How can I be. I don't know what the word means.'

One very good decision, which was made early on in our team discussions, was that we would not have any word on the screen which was not a 'teaching' word. That meant no end credits, and surprisingly, because there was no order of precedence – lighting by, sound by, written by, directed by, produced by – no pecking order: in fact there was no pecking.

On the Move was perhaps the only truly democratic series I've ever worked on. We all contributed and there were never any arguments about precedence or priority. We just got on with our respective jobs and rejoiced when the finished product, the sum of all our efforts, actually worked.

None the less the series did make some people uneasy, and the joke of the time was that we used the formula 'If you have trouble with reading and writing, please write to us here at the BBC'. Of course nothing of the kind was said or written, but we smiled at the slur and pressed on.

Looking back to what we did over fifteen years ago, nobody who was involved with any of the three series was anything but proud of what we achieved, and what is more we are all still friends today. Actors, directors, producer, animators and even the writer embrace each other on meeting, enjoy each other's company and are proud of each other's successes and sympathetic when one or other has problems.

David Hargreaves later became Head of the BBC Continuing Education Department. Barbara Derkow went into freelance production in the UK and Germany and married a doctor who works in a hospital in Cologne, where they now live.

Caroline Pick has matured into a very experienced executive producer. Bob Hoskins has starred in hit after hit from *The Long Good Friday* to *Who Framed Roger Rabbit*, and I'm writing this.

Before leaving the subject of *On the Move*, I must pay a brief tribute to Donald Gee who, playing Wise to Bob Hoskins's Morecambe, kept the ship afloat when Bob was going through a bad patch in his personal life, and who brought not only the strength of a good actor to the proceedings but intelligence, insight and humour too. If anyone deserved a medal for *On the Move*, and collectively we won awards from BAFTA and the Royal Television Society, it was Donald Gee. Long may he prosper.

*

Some of the occasional pleasures of working on television are the trips abroad.

One such came about when I was running a children's quiz for the BBC TV Saturday morning programme, *Saturday Superstore*. Through the efforts of a former secretary of mine, Angela Sharp, now a director in the BBC Children's Department, I had started making regular appearances in Noel Edmonds's *Multi Coloured Swap Shop*. The producer of this and its successor, *Saturday Superstore*, was Rosemary Gill.

For *Swap Shop* I did a junior points of view, and then a 'you send me your joke and I'll read it out' piece, and when that had run out of steam (after all you can only use 'Does God live in our bathroom?' 'No. Why?' 'Well, every morning Dad rattles the door handle and says, "Oh, God, are you still in there?"' so many times before it begins to pall) it was decided to run a quiz.

By this time Noel Edmonds had departed for richer pastures and the disc jockey Mike Read had taken over. We called the quiz 'Whatsit', as we couldn't think of anything better, advertised its coming through an entry form in *Radio Times*, and then interviewed the applicants.

It was a brisk little quiz, part general knowledge and part specialist subject, and the prize for the winner was an all-expenses-paid trip to Egypt.

In the event the likeliest winner, a girl from Slough, stumbled at the last fence and the quiz was won by a young lad from Cranleigh, Surrey. A small group of us trouped off to Cairo, filming all the way, and arrived at night. The array of battered taxis outside Cairo airport and, to the first-timer in the middle east, the depressing dinginess of the place were not terribly encouraging.

However, duly established in Shepherds Hotel and with the charming and constant cooperation of the Egyptian Tourist Board, things began to look up. We filmed the pyramids and the Sphinx, rode on camels and travelled up the Nile on a steamer. We also filmed in mosques and a bazaar, and in the Cairo museum.

Apart from armed soldiers behind ramparts of sandbags outside the Cairo Radio and Television building and the glimpses of almost unbelievable squalor off the main thoroughfares, I found Cairo very like London and the Egyptians charming and easy to get on with.

The guides had a sort of cockney bravura about them, the traffic was as bad as at home and, in fact, I felt quite at ease throughout our trip. We got back with a decent little film of our travels and I rate my trip to Cairo as one of the better 'unexpected pleasures' of my life.

Other trips to north Africa haven't been as pleasant – its combination of beggery, buggery and bureaucracy are hard to stomach. Still, if my luck holds I won't have to go to Tunisia or Morocco again, and I'll take the word of BBC reporter, Kate Adie, on the subject of Libya, as being all I need to know on the subject.

Frankly, camels, mad dictators, sand, disease and religious fundamentalism have little appeal for me.

17

Points of View

The offer to work on *Points of View* came out of the blue. Colin Ward-Lewis, a nodding acquaintance in the BBC Club bar at the Television Centre, had heard me on radio, and felt that I was the man for the job.

In the previous two years I had done an amazing amount of radio and tv. I've written elsewhere of my failures on television and of 'nearlies', shows that weren't particularly successful but weren't out-and-out flops. Two series I made for Yorkshire Television about this time fall into the *nearly* category.

The first, called *NUTS*, was produced by Ronnie Baxter and featured Roy Kinnear, Freddie Jaeger, Dave Evans, Chris Emmett and Claire Faulconbridge. It was a touch rough-and-ready but had texture and was a likeable bundle.

For our last programme Ronnie Baxter suggested that we put together a collection of out-takes: fluffs and technical foul-ups. I liked the idea and we duly finished the series showing the bits that had gone wrong. Where have I heard that before, you're asking. Well, some years later London Weekend Television put on a show called *It'll Be Alright On The Night*, which yes, got it in one – was a collection of fluffs and technical foul-ups. It was good, as its many repeats remind us. But Ronnie Baxter was first.

Next year I was asked by Yorkshire to do another series. This one was called *Took & Co.* and was produced by Vernon Lawrence. It starred Gwen Taylor and Robin Bailey, plus Chris Emmett and David Battley. It had its moments, but was more important for the fact that it put Vernon Lawrence together with Robin Bailey and Gwen Taylor, for each of whom he produced excellent programmes: Peter Tinniswood's *Tales from the Long Room* with Robin Bailey and *Duty Free* in which Gwen Taylor excelled as the wronged wife, Amy, in the long-drawn-out comedy of package-holiday makers. Yorkshire also used Chris Emmett to great advantage for several years in the curious quiz game, *3-2-1*.

I have worked for Yorkshire Television on several occasions since then – more successfully, it must be said – and have always enjoyed the experience.

About that time I was also writing jokes for Val Doonican, and much else besides. But I fell into the habit of accepting and then walking out of a lot of work, particularly book writing. I'd agree to write a book and then decide that I couldn't do it, return the advance with apologies saying that I couldn't guarantee to honour the contract. Lyn became quite cross with me for this sloppy behaviour, and after she'd given me a particularly severe wigging I promised, 'The next job I'm offered I'll accept and stick with it until they sack me.' That next job turned out to be *Points of View*, and I did stick with it for seven and a half years and two hundred and eighty-three programmes, until I *was* sacked.

But all that and much more lay in the future as I met and discussed the programme with Colin Ward-Lewis.

It was a five-minute slot scheduled for BBC1 at 10.30 pm on Friday nights, in London and the South East only. Colin would provide the script and all I had to do was come in to the studio on the Thursday before transmission and record the show, reading the script off Autocue. (Autocue is a device that by an arrangement of mirrors puts the words of the script in front of the camera lens and allows the speaker to look, with great sincerity, deep into the hearts and minds of his or her audience as he or she reads the *News*, or links *Points of View*.) Colin told me he would engage two experienced actors, used to doing voice-overs for radio and tv commercials, to read the letters.

The return of *Points of View* was duly advertised in *Radio Times* and by the continuity announcers on tv, and letters started to trickle in. It doesn't take many to fill a five-minute slot, but in the early days they weren't terribly inspiring.

Also, I found the script that I was asked to read flat and rather stilted, but soldiered on for a week or two until Colin suggested that perhaps it wouldn't be a bad idea for me to write the script. I agreed as, after all, writing was my profession and I knew what I wanted to say, or not say, about the subjects on which people were writing to the programme.

To add life to the proceedings we started using transcripts of phone calls to the BBC Duty Officer (generally wildly abusive) and quotes from television critics (generally well-reasoned abuse). Up to Christmas 1979 we struggled a bit to make the programme work, but such was the rapport between Colin Ward-Lewis, the researcher and the voice-overs – who, over the months that followed, included Michael McClain, Janie Booth, Angela Piper (Jennifer of *The Archers*), John Meeson, Marie Sutherland, Alec Bregonzi, Cass Allen and many others – that we did improve week by week, and by early in 1980 the programme had become slick, amusing and popular.

Bill Cotton, at that time Controller of BBC 1, decided in February 1980 that *Points of View* should be extended to ten minutes, go out over the whole network and be transmitted at the better time of 8.50 to 9 pm on Fridays. With occasional variations of times and days it was that way ever after.

Points of View was originally born in 1961 and first went on air on 2 October in that year. Robert Robinson was the presenter, and very good he was too. In 1965 Kenneth Robinson (no relation) took over and stuck it until 1967. There was a break until 1968 when Robert Robinson took over once again and he saw the programme through until 1971 when it went off the screen until its revival in 1979. There had been other presenters too, filling in for holidays or illness, including Alan Brien, Philip Oakes, Frank Muir and Alan Melville. Peter Bull, Beryl Cooke and Steve Race also took the Chair from time to time, as did Henry Fairlie, Harold Lang, Trevor Lucas and David Rees. Even Alan Bennett appeared on one occasion each in 1969, 1970 and 1971.

There have been many other programmes of various kinds airing viewers' grievances, including one called *Talkback*, where viewers and broadcasters met face to face in the studio. The trouble with that format, as with the contemporary *Right to Reply* on Channel Four, is that while in theory the people responsible for broadcasts are put on the spot, the debate usually degenerates into an 'Oh no I didn't – Oh yes you did' squabble, which adds nothing to our knowledge and is interesting to no one other than those involved in the argument.

It's unsurprising to me, having learnt the hard way how stupid and incompetent many of the people who are responsible for our tv are, that those same mistakes are constantly repeated, year after year, as some variation of viewer confronting management grinds its weary way to an all too predictable disaster.

It's my opinion that the *Points of View* approach is the only one which gives the viewer the maximum amount of say in what he or she thinks about tv, and gives those views maximum exposure.

Everyone knows when a programme is truly awful or when viewers' interests are being subordinated to the antics of some clown who temporarily has his hands on the control lever. No one needs said clown in the studio justifying his inanities in front of an audience who are neither trained nor experienced in studio techniques nor can really grasp the banalities that constitute the programme philosophy of these people. When top management is poor it's hardly surprising that middle and lower management are of inferior quality too. Unfortunately all too often good people are forced out by frustration, or just plain spite.

That, in a way, is what happened to Colin Ward-Lewis. After one very successful year in which he'd built *Points of View* from nothing to big success, he was told he was being replaced.

I asked the people who ran the BBC tv's Presentation Department at that time, Malcolm Walker and Janet Hoenig, whose personal likes and dislikes appeared completely to dominate any rational decision-making, why Colin was being replaced.

I was given the quickly invented excuse that it was the department's policy (it would have been news to anybody who knew the Presentation Department that it had any policy of any kind on any subject) to change producers every year so as to give as many people as possible the chance to get the experience of producing a programme rather than just making trailers for other people's programmes, which was their usual occupation.

In spite of any argument I could put up, Colin went and was replaced by Tim Simmonds, with whom I first did an Olympic Games special and then a year's very fruitful work.

To be entirely honest, Tim Simmonds was a better producer than Colin Ward-Lewis. He was a perfectionist whose editing was immaculate and whose innovations lifted the programme to new heights. He also had a super secretary/PA, Cathie Fraser, and that combination plus the often used services of director Warwick Cross made *Points of View* more vivid and visually exciting than it had been.

During Tim Simmonds's year 80–81 I put together a collection of the more interesting, outspoken and amusing letters into a book, which was published by the BBC and in consequence once published was never heard of again. Visually it was a mess, and I turn the pages today with a feeling of mounting horror, wondering how anyone could produce anything so unattractive and downright difficult to read.

However, the letters in the book are fascinating, and bearing in mind that they were written over ten years ago, I quote four, quite typical of the time:

From D.F. Spade of Grays, Essex:

I was today disgusted almost to the point of physical illness by hearing the tennis commentator John Barrett declare that John McEnroe has 'an over-developed sense of justice and fair play'. Such a sense must surely be the very last thing which would motivate this lout, whom many of us find quite nauseating enough without being told that his boorishness is, in reality, evidence of moral rectitude. Does the BBC really want to convey to its viewers – many of whom are young and impressionable – that such behaviour is not only acceptable but desirable, and if not, do we really need the consistently inane Mr Barrett?

From Anne Pettitt, Dublin:

My vote would go to Peter Alliss for his excellent coverage of the golf. He is a joy to listen to and his little comments about each player are delightful. He is never rude, but when a competitor plays a bad shot he just says 'what a dreadful shot' or 'not very well played sir' and he is just wonderful. I could listen to him all day. My second choice would go to Dan Maskell for the tennis. He only says the bare minimum and yet is most informative.

From Tamzin Later of Ilford, Essex:

Why does *Nationwide* insist on showing revolting pictures and films, when most people are having their evening meal? Today (17 October) we had delightful scenes of worms, maggots and fleas. I was fortunate enough to be merely eating chips, but I pity anyone who was eating spaghetti.

From D. Slinger, Gloucester:

> When are violence and 'horror' acceptable viewing? Answer: When they are neatly packaged with sexual deviations as pure voyeuristic entertainment. Example: Monday's film *An Investigation of Murder* about the actions and lifestyle of a deviant mass murderer.
>
> When are violence and horror not acceptable? Answer: When they are part of a serious presentation of the most vital question facing humanity. Example: *The War Game*, made by the BBC in 1965 but denied a showing ever since. Reason: The BBC knows that the establishment knows what is good for us.

All the time I was involved with *Points of View* I was constantly asked if we made up the letters. A letter from a woman in Glasgow was typical of many when she wrote: 'I thought you made the letters up until I saw my own handwriting on the screen.' There was never any need to invent, as our average, during the years I presented the programme, was a thousand letters a week.

At first they were rewritten to make it easier to paste them onto the caption cards we used in those days, and which were placed by hand on stands in front of the appropriate cameras. Later I insisted that we used the actual letters and, to my surprise, received this from a well-known graphologist, Diane Simpson:

> Watching your programme for the first time this evening – I was enchanted to see that the letters you used on the screen were 'genuine' originals rather than a TV mock up – supposedly produced to make writing more legible. There before my very eyes were your kind, impulsive, revengeful, patient, generous and curious viewer/writers. I can hardly wait for the next programme.

We invited Diane Simpson to appear in a programme later in the year, a thirty-minute special which celebrated twenty years of *Points of View*, and which also featured Robert Robinson and Kenneth Robinson. It was a programme which traced *Points of View* from its beginnings and showed how little viewers' attitudes had changed over the years.

In the many series that followed the only real changes in *Points of View* were the producers, the tiny set in which I sat and the signature tune.

Following Tim Simmonds, the programme was produced by Brian Wolstenholme. Then came Yvonne Hewett, a Canadian, who added a roll-top desk to the previously empty set and changed the signature tune to Paul McCartney's 'When I'm 64'. I wondered why until it was pointed out to me that it contains the line 'Send me a postcard, drop me a line, stating point of view'. The desk and the new tune added something to the programme and gave me the idea of putting an appropriate photograph on the top of the desk each week. The first of them celebrated the fact that John Nott, who was carrying the can for the Falklands War at the time, had walked out of an interview with Robin Day.

We put a photo of Robin on the desk with the message 'Best wishes to John'. It amused those who spotted it.

The change of signature tune brought about an amusing incident, to me at least. Paul McCartney has one of his many houses near to where I live in St John's Wood. It was Paul's habit, when staying in the neighbourhood, to breakfast with his wife Linda and the children in an excellent coffee shop in St John's Wood High Street, called Gloriette. I was taking an early morning stroll up the High Street one spring day when Paul McCartney sprang out of the doorway of Gloriette and said, 'Excuse me, can I have your autograph?' He then fell about laughing. When he'd recovered from his mirth he explained, 'That's happened to me so often and I've always wanted to do it somebody else'. He introduced me to his wife and children, and said some kind things about *Points of View*, and we went our separate ways. I must admit that although it had been a joke on his part I glowed for weeks at the thought of being asked for my autograph by Paul McCartney.

Yvonne Hewett's year came and went, and next to bat was Carol White, who was sweet, warm and giggly and who added potted plants to the set, making it more home-like. She and her husband, Johnny Black, pop music journalist, were trying for a baby at the time and she would appear round the Points of View office door, mid-morning, looking slightly bedraggled, as if she'd tumbled out of bed – which, as it turned out, she had. She duly became pregnant, had a daughter, Joanna, and then a son, William, left the BBC and set up home in the West Country.

My next producer was Bernie Newman, a no-nonsense technician who simplified the set, commissioned an animated opening graphic to the show and produced briskly for the statutory year before handing over to Penny Mills. She commissioned a brand new (and extremely ugly) set and new opening graphics, which I frankly didn't care for. It was a fairly uneventful year.

Until then the routine was for *Points of View* to take a summer break of three months while the sporting scene (cricket, athletics, etc.) was at its height, but around this time Michael Grade, fresh from his failures elsewhere, joined the BBC as Controller BBC 1 (and Managing Director elect). He decided that *Points of View* should run twelve months of the year, and I was asked how many programmes I wished to do. I said I'd like a seven- to eight-week break in the summer, and this was agreed. My substitutes the first year of the new regime were Andrew Sachs (3 weeks) and Nanette Newman (4 weeks), and in the second year, by which time the producer was Vicki Marriot, Anne Robinson took over the hot seat while I had a holiday.

That she was a success there is no doubt, and on my return to the programme Lyn was summoned to meet Malcolm Walker and Janet Hoenig to discuss further developments. Lyn had for many years looked after all my business affairs and had regular meetings with Walker and/or Hoenig when things had, from time to time, become sticky.

In August 1986, on my way home from holiday, in a sleeping berth in the train chugging north to Boulougne from Narbonne, and unable to sleep, I reviewed my time with *Points of View*, my promise to Lyn to stick it out and my general feelings about my career. I was 58 years old, I'd had a hectic decade in radio and television and I wanted a break. I'd had good times and much patronage from the top echelons of the BBC. Sir Ian Trethowan had been a keen supporter, as had Sir Michael (later Lord) Swann, the Chairman, his successor, George Howard, and *his* successor, Stuart Young. Stuart Young and I had a particular affinity as he'd been to school in Finchley and had actually been in the same class as Marty Feldman. Down the line, however, there were rumblings of discontent. I always took the view that I was defending the viewers' right to say whatever they thought, but many producers and Heads of Departments felt that I should only quote letters favourable to them. The support of the people at the top of the organisation kept these wolves at bay –

Light Entertainment and Sport were particularly thin-skinned – but when Stuart Young died tragically of cancer and Alasdair Milne was sacked I knew it wouldn't be long before I too got my marching orders. Besides that, I had become bored with *Points of View*. The constant change of producers, the refusal to make changes which would have stopped the programme from sagging, the petty bureaucracy and the sheer sloppiness of the Presentation Department – even the dirty, cluttered office gave me the pip. I had no quarrel with the people who read the letters, and we had, in my opinion, reached a perfect combination of voice and personality in the quartet, who liked each other, mocked each other but related well both at work and socially.

They were Anna Barry, Nicolette McKenzie, John Marsh the Radio 2 Newsreader and the ever-present Michael McClain. The other ever-present member of the team was the Autocue operator Patricia Ball. She's a lanky charmer with a slight cockney accent mixed oddly with touches of Sloane Square. She's blessed with a good sense of humour and she quickly became a friend of us all. We were delighted to share our recording day with her as she gossiped cheerfully during tea breaks, and professionally she was unfailingly helpful to me. Patricia's great skill is to get on with practically everybody (the only exception being an 80s lady newsreader whom she couldn't stand). She's a dear, and a dear friend to Lyn and me, now parted from Autocue but working for a similar outfit called Autoprompt.

My last producer, Peter Gould, who had replaced Vicki Marriot (to my mind one of the best producers I had) was not my sort of person. He was an ex-Army Captain who shortly after becoming producer of *Points of View* departed for a job with Super Channel, an early runner in the satellite market, so I didn't have to bear him long.

To cap everything I'd received an angry abusive letter from Michael Grade complaining about a newspaper article I'd written criticising some elements of the BBC output. All in all I felt that I'd had enough of BBC television and on that train journey north through France I decided that when my current contract ended, at Christmas 1986, I would do no more.

When Lyn met Malcolm Walker and was told that after

Christmas my services would no longer be required, she said, 'Well, Barry will be pleased. He doesn't want to do any more.'

The whole thing passed off quietly and a large chunk of my working life, almost the longest run I've ever been involved in, was over.

People still stop me in the street and ask when I'm going back. I don't believe I ever will go back. It's more fun going on to new situations, and there are many things both in my working and private life that I would like to accomplish. I might even take up playing the trumpet again. Who knows, I might get it right this time.

Index